D0895354

PUBLIC-SECTOR MARKETING

Wiley Series on Business Strategy
WILLIAM A. COHEN

PUBLIC-SECTOR MARKETING

A GUIDE FOR
PRACTITIONERS

Larry L. Coffman

JOHN WILEY & SONS
New York · Chichester · Brisbane · Toronto · Singapore

Library of Congress Cataloging in Publication Data:

Coffman, Larry L.
    Public-sector marketing.

    (Wiley series on business strategy)
    Bibliography: p.
    Includes index.
    1. Government marketing. I. Title. II. Series.

JF1525.M37C64   1986   350.81'9   86-9216
ISBN 0-471-01161-4

Printed in the United States of America

10 9 8 7 6 5 4 3 2 1

To those with a grand goal
and the perseverance to pursue it.

Foreword

Managing in the public sector is no easy task nowadays. Tightened funding at all levels of government is coupled with rhetoric from the right of the political spectrum that demeans the work of many public agencies and caricatures nonuniformed public managers as "unresponsive bureaucrats."

Certainly, there is waste and unresponsiveness to be found in all types of organizations, both for-profit and not-for-profit. Similarly, excellence, innovation, and creativity are not confined to the private sector. As Tom Peters and Nancy Austin illustrated in *Passion for Excellence* (Random House, 1985) and as Charles B. Weinberg and I showed in *Marketing for Public and Nonprofit Managers* (Wiley, 1984), there are many examples of successful public services at all levels of government.

Underlying characteristics of such organizations include a clearly defined mission, service to customers that reflects an understanding of their needs, and recognition of the role of employees in contributing to customer satisfaction. These are all characteristics associated with successful marketers who recognize that their organizations—like most public agencies—are in business for the long haul.

Although many public agencies have not had a strong marketing orientation in the past, this situation is now changing. Part of the challenge faced by marketing managers and chief executives alike is to market the very concept of marketing within their own organizations. Without a clear internal understanding of what the marketing function is, and of what marketing efforts can and cannot do, no public agency can hope to develop and implement effective marketing strategies.

Public-Sector Marketing will appeal not only to marketing practitioners but also to those who hold other positions in public management and need to understand what marketing is all about.

Talking about marketing and actually doing it successfully are two very different things; Larry Coffman is very good at both. He spent more than a decade as manager of marketing with the Metro bus system serving metropolitan Seattle. During that time he helped to elevate public transportation in Seattle from a second-class service to a model for the North American transit industry. Ridership more than doubled in Washington State's most populous area as the public responded to service improvements and innovations resulting from Coffman's ambitious and intelligent approach to marketing.

Now a publishing executive and lecturer, Larry Coffman has drawn on his experience as an international consultant, as well as his years at Metro, to develop this "user-friendly" guide to achieving positive marketing results in all types of public agencies. He's realistic about the internal and external obstacles with which public sector marketers must deal (after all, he's had to deal with them himself), but shows how to come to grips with these problems.

Managers, chief executives, and board members alike can benefit from Coffman's insights. He gets to the heart of effective marketing, emphasizing that marketing goes far beyond just advertising and publicity efforts. This concise and readable book should be of great value to any public agency that is concerned with delivering its services in a more responsive and efficient manner.

CHRISTOPHER H. LOVELOCK

Cambridge, Massachusetts

Series Preface

Peter Drucker said, "The future will not just happen if one wishes hard enough. It requires decision—now. It imposes risk—now. It requires action—now. It demands allocation of resources, and above all, human resources—now." The Wiley Series on Business Strategy is published to assist managers with the task of creating the future in their organizations.

Creation of the future requires application of the art and science of strategy. Strategy comes from the Greek word "strategia," which means generalship. It has clear military roots defining how a general deploys the available forces and resources to achieve military objectives. But business and military strategy, though similar, are not identical. Business strategy is the allocation of resources to achieve a differential advantage at the time and place of decisive importance. "Resources" may be human, they may be financial, promotional, have to do with unique know-how, or have a psychological emphasis. But to be effective, these resources must be concentrated so as to be superior where it counts. This achievement is the essence of any successful business strategy and the theme of the series.

The series will investigate strategy in all of its many facets in business including marketing, management, planning, finance, communications, promotional activities, leadership, corporate culture—to note only those topics under preparation or planned. Its aim is to equip the practicing manager with the techniques and tools he or she will need for the most competitive and exciting period in business of all time.

WILLIAM A. COHEN
Series Editor

Preface

Public-sector marketing has a muddled image at best. This book seeks to make a clear statement about what it is and does—as a platform for improvement. Here is an exciting and rewarding career field. Yet it has little standing because it is the subject of misunderstanding and malpractice. That's not pessimism. It's a base of reality from which to move on with optimism.

The audience is threefold: practicing and prospective public-sector marketers, nonmarketers in the public sector, and private-sector marketers. There's something in the book for all—whether you're out to learn, to figure out what those marketing people are really trying to do, to compare notes with your own experience, or a little of each.

The obstacles in the path of progress are real and substantial, but they can be overcome in time. The challenge is to clarify what this special business is all about, to attract top people to it, and to hold them once they're there. With all that, an improved image will follow:

The obstacle course begins with a definition.

1. People know planners produce plans. Operators deliver service. Maintenance people maintain it. Accountants count money. Marketing, in contrast, is used as a synonym for every activity in the communications realm from advertising to sales promotion to public relations to community relations—and some others besides.

2. Hence, when an ad appears for a marketing position, it attracts an amazing array of candidates with minimal marketing credentials.

3. This, in turn, opens what is called "marketing" to criticism from policy boards, chief executives, peers, and the public.

4. As a result, the majority of those hired under false pretenses move on within a short time, for a variety of reasons.

5. Finally, the quality and image of marketing suffers still further as the self-defeating spiral continues.

The first step on the long journey to respectability is to prepare practitioners more fully and give them the perspective needed to perform at peak effectiveness. I hope this book will help. The second is to do more systematic marketing planning and more powerful promotion. And the third is to deliver results consistently. That's what the public-sector marketing business should be about.

All marketing is a blend of science and art. Both are integral to a marketing process that begins with planning, continues with promotion, and ends with evaluation—only to start over with planning in a continuing cycle. Public-sector marketing is set apart because it bears a special responsibility to treat the total public as "owners" of the business, not just those who use the service.

There is good cause for optimism about the future of public-sector marketing. The era of instant information will continue to heighten competition for the public's attention and support. This makes more and better marketing mandatory. Until now, there has been little written on public-sector marketing from the practitioner's perspective. Perhaps that should not be too surprising in view of the obstacles outlined earlier.

You'll find the traditional textbook and marketing theory and terminology used here, but in a practical context, aided by lots of examples. Relegating detailed definitions to the comprehensive Glossary helped to keep the chapters shorter and the pace more rapid.

With the step-by-step guidance from this book, you can tackle any public-sector marketing assignment. The checklist (see Appendix A) provides a takeoff point for improving or initiating any public-sector marketing program.

While public-sector marketing may be misunderstood by many, the spiritual rewards are great (and the pay is getting better). The chance to make a difference in the community or the country is perhaps the main magnet to public service today—and for the future. As a front-line function, marketing is second to none in opportunity.

Use this book on the job—or in preparing for one—with the confidence that it contains the perspective and experience of those who've been there—and achieved good results. I'm indebted to a number of my colleagues who lent their time and expertise to the final product. They include Ann Downs, Lynn Flanders, Dr. David Lingwood, Reza Moinpour, Ray Shea, Monte Solkover, Dean Tonkin and, especially, Ken Gollings and Christopher Lovelock. This book was enhanced through their many contributions.

I would also like to acknowledge the wealth of information obtained from my former professor James L. Heskett's book *Marketing* (Macmillan, 1976) and Irving J. Shapiro's *Dictionary of Marketing Terms* (Littlefield, Adams, 1981).

LARRY L. COFFMAN

Kirkland, Washington
August 1986

Contents

PUBLIC-SECTOR MARKETING

1

public-sector marketing

WHAT IT *IS*

How could a fast-growing field like public-sector marketing remain so unrecognized and unappreciated for so long? This is a good question. The answer lies in lack of definition, lack of a disciplined approach, and lack of practitioner's trained in—and committed to—public-sector marketing per se.

The very phrase public-sector marketing is a marriage of two widely misunderstood terms. "Public sector" conjures up some fuzzy notions about bureaucrats and tax-supported budgets; "marketing" is among the most misused words in the English language. People persist in using it, wrongly, as a synonym for advertising, public relations, and most other categories of the communications field.

PUBLIC SECTOR: A TO Z

The blurred picture of the public sector is all the more mystifying in view of the fact that about half the employed people in the United States work in the public sector. (The American military is the western world's biggest business.) As a check on your own perception, scan the illustrative A to Z list of public sector organizations in Figure 1. (The sample goals are to help zero in on a definition.) All such organizations have the following in common:

1. They are financed in whole or in part by public tax dollars or donations, giving them a responsibility to respond to the public that goes beyond the private-sector responsibility to be a "good corporate citizen."

2. They consider their authorized (and hopefully balanced) budget the bottom line, unlike the private sector, which measures financial success by the size of the profit or return on investment (ROI).

3. They offer service as the product, whether tangible

ORGANIZATION/ AGENCY	GOALS
Associations (nonprofit)	More members
Blood banks	More donors
Colleges and universities	More students
Disabled homes	Public support
Energy agencies	Energy conservation
Fire departments	Public cooperation
Garbage dumps	Neighborhood acceptance
Hospitals	Full occupancy
Information centers	Fewer telephone calls
Jails	Better community image
Kitchen services	Customer satisfaction
Libraries	Fewer overdue books
Museums	More memberships
Narcotics-control agencies	Public support
"Olympics" organizations	More contributions
Political candidates	Getting elected
Quartermaster Corps	More recruits
Recreational agencies	Vandalism control
State police	Fewer highway fatalities
Transit systems	More riders
Urban-planning agencies	Master-plan adoption
Vocational schools	More enrollment
Welfare agencies	Fewer recipients
X-ray laboratories	Public acceptance
Youth centers	Community support
Zoos	More attendance

Figure 1. An A to Z list of public-sector organization and goals.

(food) or intangible (education); in the private sector, the product is either service (consultant advice) or a manufactured item (automobiles).

4. They are seeking to increase (or in some cases decrease) the use of their services, while building their public favor and financial base.

    (**Note:** nonprofit organizations fit the definition of public sector, too, primarily because they are working from an authorized budget—usually supported by public donations—and providing service as the product.)

MARKETING DEFINED

So much for the easy half of the definition. Now for marketing, and its meaning in the public-sector context. The definitions of marketing are as numerous as the number of speeches, articles, and books on the subject, whether we're talking about the public *or* the private sector.

Here's still another definition, incorporating the five "rights," which doubles as a model for marketing success: Marketing is getting the right service to the right markets at the right price by the right means at the right time ("right," in all cases, is a judgment call that is the crux of the marketing practitioner's job).

And it must be pointed out that marketing is *not:*

- Research
- Media advertising
- Sales promotion
- Customer service

- Direct sales
- Distribution

Marketing is *all* of these functions, *not* to be used synonymously or interchangeably with any of them (i.e., marketing is *not* public relations and vice versa).

In the public sector, marketing is the two-way catalyst for change between the design of service and the public, as shown in Figure 2. The circular, and continuing, process begins with the joint marketing/planning service design,

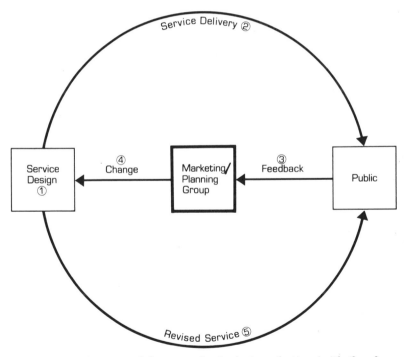

Figure 2. A diagram of the central role that marketing (with the planning group) *should* play in design and revision of service in response to public feedback, beginning with initial design (1) through revisions in response to feedback (5).

followed by service delivery, accommodation of public feedback, redesign (change) as needed, and redelivery.

Having a strong role in service design sounds relatively
simple and straightforward, however, what usually happens is one of the following:

1. All of the so-called marketing activities are really
    only one-way communications with the public, and
    the chief executive designs the service with no ac-
    commodation of change.

2. Same as number 1, but the planners design the ser-
    vice.

3. The marketing group is in competition with the plan-
    ners, operators, and accountants for control over ser-
    vice design, with the chief executive in the veto role.

There are many variations on this list, but the net effect
is still the same. Organizational structure (the focus of
Chapter 2) is a critical determinant of whether you'll be
able to implement the process shown in Figure 2. Another
is the quality of your annual marketing plan, which is the
marketer's main means of prompting concerted and continuing movement toward organizational goals and objectives.
Progress is directly dependent on the resources and resolve
that propel the plan.

The matter of whether marketing is given the resources
to become a true two-way connection and catalyst for
change rests almost completely in the chief executive's
hands. The crucial question is how much authority he or
she is willing to give you and how much confidence your
superior has in you to help guide the service design.

With the complete backing of your boss—and the policy
board—any obstacles will quickly disappear. The marketer
who's getting support—even strokes—is certain to grow in

confidence, competence, and commitment to the job. If your situation is promising but could be better—persevere. And if you have a good situation, don't take it for granted. Foster it with communication and candid reports of your progress—or lack of it.

The major thrust of marketing, in most cases, is to increase the use of service. Yet it sometimes may be necessary to decrease the use of a service, or some facet of the service. This is called demarketing.

An example of demarketing an entire service is the about-face forced on the energy industry as power became less plentiful in most parts of the United States. Instead of selling all-electric kitchens they had to shift to a message of conservation. An example of demarketing a facet of service is seeking to divert bus patrons from overuse of costly telephone information to less-costly information sources, such as timetables and bus stop schedule signs. One bus system faced with this problem received good results simply by adding the words "New Rider" in front of its information number—thereby politely telling the current riders to use other information sources.

THE FIVE RIGHTS

All five elements of the marketing definition/success model have much depth of meaning. However, the first—right service—has an added dimension of importance. Without it, you shouldn't proceed.

Right Service

After World War II, chrome-laden gas guzzlers carried General Motors (GM) to the pinnacle of corporate sales success. Three decades later, GM still was trying to sell the same type of cars in the face of a flood of trim, economical foreign imports, even though their own research recommended otherwise. Finally, all the automakers got in step with the public demand and their own research—and sales rebounded dramatically.

This illustrates again why research-based marketing must have a strong hand in guiding the design of the service (product) to be sold. For years, the so-called marketers in the auto-making business were only advertising or selling a predetermined product, not marketing a product in the true two-way sense of the word.

If you don't have—or listen to—good research, the result will be the same as with the automakers—a misuse of resources. For example, in the public sector, this means providing lots of bus service at times and places people don't want to go, offering school courses that are outdated, or proposing a master land-use plan that flies in the face of prevailing trends. (Of course, there will be exceptions, but you must shape the service to meet the majority needs.)

If you are separate and equal (or unequal) in relation to the planning person or group, and let them shape the service without research, you're abandoning the right to call what you're doing marketing. At that point it is only sales or public relations work on a product that you had no hand in shaping. You have responsibility but no control.

Your task is to get the market research done and fully incorporated into the service design—or redesign—immediately. Do it whether you have no, partial, or complete control over it. If at first (or second or third) you don't succeed—persevere.

Right Markets

Research also is the bridge to the second element of the marketing definition—the right markets—that portion (or segment) of the existing or potential users you are trying to reach with your message.

Since the marketer is always attempting to reach multiple markets, you need to segment them. Markets are segmented in one of several ways: demographically (who they are), geographically (where they are), psychographically (how they behave), and type of response to service (user/ nonuser). Market segmentation is the key to cost-effective targeting of your markets, and the more precisely you can do it the more successful you'll be. (More about segmentation in Chapter 5.)

Right Price

After service design, pricing poses the next greatest challenge for the public-sector marketer. In the private sector, there is usually no argument with marketing's lead role in pricing. That's because in bottom-line ROI businesses, marketing is mandatory. And they realize pricing is a prime consideration in people's decisions to buy. In the public sector, marketing's shaky standing and the highly political nature of fees/rates/fares and the like make pricing hard to get hold of—much less control.

The impact of public-sector pricing decisions is unquestioned. For example, increases in community college tuitions in the early 1980s caused a rapid 20 percent decrease in enrollment. Rising postal rates have been a significant factor in the growth of competition (United Postal Service, Federal Express, etc.). And energy costs are a prime consideration in the location or relocation of major tax-producing industries.

However pricing is done in your agency, you cannot—must not—cede total control of it to others. Pricing is an inextricable part of the service you're seeking to shape and charged with selling.

Right Means

As segmentation and pricing are part of the science of marketing, the right means is part of the art. Means covers both the promotional media mix and the channels of distribution you choose to employ in delivering your message. Media planning and distribution are two of the most overlooked and underestimated tools available to the marketer. Appreciate and use them. Like any art, it takes much practice to become skilled in directing the delivery of your promotional message. (More about this in Chapter 7.)

Right Time

The fifth element—timing—is closely related to the means of communicating the message. It is obvious that the best brochure or television spot in the world can't work to its best advantage if it's late or ill-timed.

Less obvious is when or how heavily you begin marketing a service. The worst thing you can do with a bad product is promote it. So the first step is to make sure you have a product worth marketing. If not, work on improving your service and keep a low profile until it's good enough to promote.

For example, if you're taking over as the marketer for a zoo that is rundown and broke, don't begin with a multimedia blitz, even if you can afford it. It probably will be your first and last act on that job. Working on the product could mean things like promoting a bond issue for needed improvements, pushing for an upgrade in the appearance of the grounds, training staff, and improving the basic information aids, such as directional signs and brochures.

Timing, once the product is presentable, also relates to the sequencing of promotional campaign waves and flights. (See Glossary.) In the case of the zoo, the campaign should seek to attract customers during the summer months when people are most likely to visit the zoo. Conversely, if you're marketing a transit system geared to carrying commuters to and from work, the summer-vacation months are not the time to spend heavily in paid media.

In both examples, however, some promotion is needed in the off-season to provide continuity between campaign waves. If the media and other promotional pieces are allowed to hit helter-skelter over a typical two- to three-month campaign wave period, much of the impact is lost. That's bad, and it's the fault of the marketer-in-charge.

THE MARKETING FUNCTIONS

The scope and structure of the marketing group differ in every organization to some degree, contributing to the problems with definition. However, the marketing functions—though called by other names or categorized differently—are: customer service, research, advertising, sales promotion, public relations, and distribution.

The marketer's job is to orchestrate these functions and their output in a way that achieves the two-way link with the customer and gets the right service to the right markets at the right price by the right means at the right time. That's a tall order, but that's what a marketer's about.

Something's wrong if you promote a service the public doesn't want. Or if you don't deliver on what you're promoting. Or if your people were unaware of promises made in the paid media that involve them. Those are the discordant sounds of musicians tuning up—not the sweet music that's possible with a marketer performing effectively in the conductor's role. (See Chapter 7.)

Achievement of your ultimate goal (selling your service) begins with the basics—customer service and research:

Customer Service

Your prime responsibility is customer service, even as you work on the overall service and research base. People who buy your product take precedence. Period. This function centers on telephone information and complaint-handling, contacts at walk-in centers and basic printed information. There is no limit to the total list of special services that any public-sector organization might conceive to make its service easier to use or more suited to the needs of the customer. (Chapter 3 is devoted to a full discussion of this fundamental function.)

Research

The absolute foundation of marketing is research, because you can't know the public's expectations and desires for service without it. Chapter 4 goes into the various research methods (personal interviews, telephone and mail surveys, focus groups, intercept interviews, and recognition and recall testing) and their uses. The methods mentioned are primary research. Even if you can't afford one or a combination of these just now, research from already-available sources (secondary research) is better than nothing—

and, in fact, should always be the starting point in your research effort. Secondary sources include census reports, surveys by similar agencies, and local planning-organization data.

Advertising

Broadcast and print media for which you pay production and time/space/special-distribution costs is advertising. Don't—repeat—don't embark on expensive advertising (especially the production of television spots) without a commitment from your superior to a sustained and strong media budget. One-shot campaigns (or those where there are high-quality television and radio spots but insufficient money to run them) are the quickest way to waste money. Moreover, it's as irresponsible as not using good research once you get it. (Much more about advertising (promotion) in Chapter 6.)

Sales Promotion

The gamut of events, merchandising materials, and specialty items available to the marketer is sales promotion. Once produced, the pieces or activities are distributed or implemented largely by your staff. The direct public contact involved is a healthy by-product.

Whatever your budget, look for cooperative promotional opportunities with partners in either the public or private sectors who have mutual markets. For example, get merchants to offer discounts or bonuses on their goods or services with the presentation of a monthly admission pass. Another idea for beefing-up slim budgets is getting supporters to sponsor the purchase of equipment or facilities. Cities and colleges have offered citizens and alumni the chance to sponsor everything from decorative manhole covers to microscopes. A Seattle zoo, in a clever takeoff on the concept, offered a "Zoo Parent" program (Figure 3) where the patron received a framed picture of the adopted pet in return for a donation (prices ranged from $15 for a prairie dog to $1,500 for a snow leopard).

Direct sales (including automatic selling from vending machines), a staple function in private-sector marketing, is in this category as well. The amount of direct-selling activity in the public sector varies from very infrequent to extremely intense—in the case of military recruiters or association executives seeking new members.

Public Relations

In its purest form, public relations (PR) involves contacts with newspapers and broadcast media and often is the sole and so-called marketing activity. The role of the media-relations aspect of the PR function is to project an agency's public "face" and "personality" and help to preserve or polish the total image. Public Relations is one-way, with no influence or control on the shape of service. Although PR may rely on other areas of marketing from time to time (like research and advertising), they are not inherent in public relations. Public relations can help snowball the impact of a paid-media campaign. Free-media events (e.g., news conferences or special ceremonies) can generate positive media coverage (in the majority of cases) that would cost tens of thousands of dollars to duplicate in paid advertising. And the message is more believable coming from the media than from actors or announcers you hired to deliver it. The only drawback is that you can't control the message and timing of its delivery with PR, as you can with paid

Figure 3. The logo for the "Zoo Parent" program. (Reproduced with permission of the Woodland Park Zoo.)

advertising. (The same is true of television spots run as public-service announcements.)

The media-relations or public-information unit also usually handles internal communications through media like newsletters (house organs), bulletin boards, and special presentations, such as publications or video productions. If the agency is spread in many locations, this activity becomes critical in establishing and maintaining unity in the organization.

There's a facet of PR in the public sector called community relations that is essential because of the public ownership of the service. This is the point of continuing contact with various public-interest groups. It's also where impasses between a public agency and the opponents of a particular project are dealt with—or should be. This work calls for the proverbial patience of Job. No text can provide simple solutions to the complex issues that face public agencies in the new world of instant information and active consumerism. The best hope is to have your act together so that you can bring a unified effort to bear on the particular problem—whether it be responding to neighborhood opposition to the siting of a landfill (garbage dump) or outrage against jet noise in the airport landing-approach zone. Most important, keep the response in line with the over-all policies of the organization, because concessions made in one area can have serious negative repercussions in others. For example, if you offer extensive and costly buffering amenities with the new landfill, you can expect like requests from those living near other existing and unbuffered sites. If you're prepared to do that, fine, just think about the ramifications of each concession. At the same time, don't use the fact that you'll have to do something for others as an excuse to do nothing when action is called for. That's the mark of a tired bureaucrat, not an aggressive marketer.

Government relations is still another facet of the PR function that is most effective as part of the marketing group. This encompasses all of the contacts with government and political people key to your agency's well-being. Divorcing the lobbying activity from marketing increases the potential for sending mixed messages to the all-important political audience.

These units of PR, along with media-relations, should share responsibility for labor relations with top management and the operating group, if your agency is unionized. A union strike or slowdown can have a traumatic effect on your entire marketing effort. Keep a close eye on union–management relations at all times, not just during the tense period when a new contract is being negotiated.

A hybrid of government relations is the relatively new

field of public affairs, which has been described as the "intersection of public and private decision-making." This is where the interests of large corporations, in matters like utility rates, environmental-impact statements, and annexations are dealt with—and hopefully resolved—before conflicts between the public and private sectors can arise. If there's a distinction between government relations and public affairs, it's that the latter takes a broader view of public policy, while the former is on the firing line.

This is also an appropriate place to put the graphics team. Photography, graphic arts, and audio-visual support are all means of conveying the public face and personality of an agency. While most every agency will buy such services from outside shops, it is virtually mandatory to have an in-house graphics capability. And it's most important that it be in the marketing group—otherwise much valuable time is lost coordinating and cajoling far beyond what is necessary if the marketer has control. It's better to direct than debate.

Distribution

Little attention is paid to distribution, yet it is vital to placing your message into the hands and minds of the target audiences. A major decision here is whether to set up an in-house distribution unit for some materials or to rely entirely on outside distribution houses for everything. Your final decision will depend largely on the complexity of your channels of distribution.

Poor or ill-timed distribution is too often the Achilles heel of what otherwise would have been a successful project. Since distribution is the last step in the process, distributors sometimes end up like the person at the end of the line in the old ice-skating game of crack-the-whip. The only way to prevent being left out in the cold is with good planning and coordination.

Internal Readiness

Internal readiness is not a function—but a state of being. It's so easy to get caught up in the functions of putting a project together that when it's time for the kick-off, those you're relying on to make it work are the last to find out what's going on (even after the customer in extreme cases). Your organization—particularly the front-liners like telephone operators and counter clerks—should know at least a week before the big campaign or event breaks what it's all about—in detail. Special training may be required as well. (Role-playing of actual customer contacts is a good technique.)

Readiness begins with the face your agency puts forth. Customers notice your people first. Uniforms are appropriate for counter clerks, guides, distribution personnel and, of course, large service forces like fire fighters, police officers, and bus drivers. Uniform colors and graphics should be coordinated to help present a clean and consistent public image. Hopefully the nonuniformed employees have the pride to dress appropriately in order to avoid the need for any kind of dress code.

General training is another key to readiness and has much to do with how the personality of your agency is perceived. There is no replacement for well-trained people and no place in a progressive agency for the ill-trained—especially those in constant contact with the customer. (A strong case can be made for putting the training function in the marketing group, too, since it is the front-line group.) Besides thorough training, be sure your staff members have the necessary—and best possible—equipment to do the job. The disruptive influence of something as small as not having enough pencils (with erasers) is amazing.

Readiness relies on good morale. And nothing tops the pride of being part of a first-rate agency. On a practical level, employee contests can be a good morale builder, but the legal difficulties in paying for prizes or cash bonuses with public tax dollars makes this a problem. A surrogate of sorts is the merit-pay system, based on a formal management-by-objectives (MBO) program. This is widely used and accepted in the public sector. The better you do on your objectives, the better your pay. Recognition is another good technique. This can take the form of selecting an employee of the month or year, or featuring employees in advertisements—or both. Special perks like a reserved parking space can be given as a reward and reinforcement of the recognition.

All of the preparatory work you do with internal staff should be aimed at gearing them to respond reflexively, instinctively—and willingly—in routine matters so they have maximum time for creative matters.

THE BIG TABOOS

Even with chief executives and boards who have a good understanding of marketing, there's difficulty in getting funds for media advertising—especially television. Many public/political leaders have a genuine and deep-seated concern about spending public tax dollars for anything but basic customer services—an essential function of marketing to be sure, but only part of the whole.

The impact of advertising will be debated forever, in the private as well as the public sector. The proper course is to use the appropriate advertising media and to measure the results in relation to stated objectives. Even so, it's difficult to get approval for paid advertising in the public sector because of its visibility and cost.

Paid television advertising is usually the biggest taboo because it's highly visible and the cost to produce good-quality television spots and run them for any length of time costs a minimum of several hundred thousand dollars. However, radio also can be taboo, since it's high-profile—though far less expensive than television. Politicians on your board know how much media advertising costs. They sometimes buy it themselves.

There have been situations where broadcast media—other than public service announcements (PSAs)—were taboo under any circumstances, yet the board was fully supportive of campaigns featuring slick full-color printed materials that cost as much or more than a comparable broadcast-oriented campaign. If you get a large budget for print—it's certainly better than nothing.

However, it's your job to convince the board and your superior that putting the high-profile parts of the media-mix off limits is like tying one arm behind your back. It's one thing to give good service and take good care of the customers you have. But there also is a responsibility to fully use the service capacity—whatever the form of your service—that public funds have built or bought. This oftens requires reaching large numbers of potential customers, which can be done most effectively with broadcast media—in combination with print and sales promotion.

A caution here. With any television station and most radio stations you'll get so-called waste circulation, where the coverage goes beyond your service area. You'll have to decide whether you're willing to accept the waste in order to make the impact. If you're still adamant about some television, it may be time to consider producing PSAs. Even these can cost more than $20,000 to produce, so it's important to get agreement from at least one television station that it will run the spots when produced. Cable station videotext billboards offer a super-low-cost television alternative, with a corresponding drop in impact compared with commerical television stations.

Either as a last resort where there is no marketing budget, or as a budget supplement, find projects that *generate* revenues that can be returned to the marketing coffers. (This may take some negotiation with your friends in accounting—even if you find such a project—because they like to put all revenues into the general fund, not your account.) In the transit industry, bus-card advertising is a big revenue source for many systems. Likewise advertising in route timetables and on bus shelters. Usually these arrangements are through outside contractors who return a percentage of gross revenues to your agency (and hopefully your marketing budget). Another way to extend your budget is to accept advertising in your newsletter or other promotional materials.

Whatever your budget circumstance, make sure to follow two rules when spending public tax dollars: (1) never be frivolous or self-serving and (2) always assess and report the results. (See Chapter 8 for a discussion on reporting results.) Frivolous and self-serving is a slide show or report telling how wonderful the marketing program is—rather than how it's contributing to the success of your service.

The preparation of a thorough, well-written marketing plan provides your best opportunity to achieve support for any or all aspects of your marketing program, including paid advertising. The comprehensive written report is far more compelling and convincing than attempting to proceed verbally or with only selected pieces of the plan reduced to writing. In short, the written plan is a *must* if you are to have any hope of real success.

2

organization

STUDY THE STRUCTURE

Many marketers make a big mistake—not studying the organizational structure. Especially if it's their first job— they leap right in, paying little attention to how the agency is organized. If things are bad enough, it's grounds for not accepting a job to begin with. If you're already there, here's hoping you have the ideal situation (described at the end of this chapter). In any case, study the structure closely.

For some reason, public agencies seem to be the last to get the word on the importance of structure. Sports is the model. Take pro football for instance. The first weeks of preseason are spent organizing the personnel into offensive, defensive, and special teams. On each of the teams, great care is given to placing the right player in the right position—and making each unit feel vital to the team's success; balance among the three breeds self-confidence, mutual respect—and winning teams.

When the marketing group is outweighed heavily by one or more peer groups in responsibilities and authority, it tells the marketing staff that they are less important—and they suffer, along with the effectiveness of the entire agency team. The negative impact of structural imbalance on employees can't be overstated.

TWO STRUCTURES

There's a world of difference between a structure in which the span of control covers six to eight top-level groups and one where it's consolidated into three or four groups, balanced in responsibilities and authority. A pyramidal structure, like the one illustrated in Figure 4, more nearly balances the importance of each major group. "Scatteration" leads to imbalance and concentration of real power at the top—in one or two individuals.

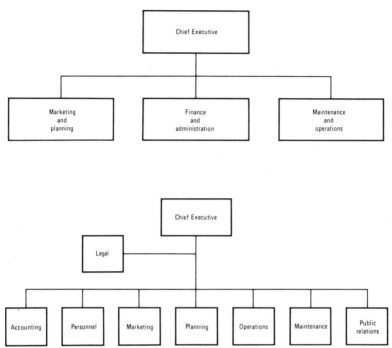

Figure 4. Diagrams of two basic organizational structures encountered in the public sector: (*upper*) pyramidal and (*lower*) scatteration, which is typical, is made even worse from a marketing viewpoint by the separation of public relations (information) into a parallel group.

The pyramidal approach will always be better for marketing. The more groups, the more likely marketing will become a weak member among many stronger groups. The real problem, however, is with the scatter approach that dramatically reduces marketing's ability to influence the shape of service. With consolidation and balance, you're ahead at the start.

Whether you're the sole marketer, head of the marketing group, or part of the group, the message on striving for a pro-marketing structure is for you. As shown in Figure 4, structures a and b represent the difference between being in the middle of the action (a), or spending much of the time on the sidelines (b). It's up to you to work for change if the structure is less than ideal. And the only way to do this is to work directly with your superior.

HOW TO COPE

Assuming the structure you're in, or about to become a part of, is more related to example b than a, you have some work to do. This is sensitive business for many reasons. Chief executives generally have their own ideas about why it should be set up that way. Peers are sensitive about their own positions, especially if a move that helps you will in any way downgrade them. And working on the organizational structure is not generally considered to be in your job description, unless someone asks for your opinion.

So make the last point the starting point. After you've gotten to know your boss fairly well, voice your concerns and ask if you may talk about them in detail. Meanwhile, you should draft out some alternatives and your view of the advantages and disadvantages of each. If you're asked to present your ideas, don't expect an instant response or decision. This is an important matter that needs to be considered from all sides.

Another avenue is through organizational studies by an outside consultant. If such a study is initiated, seek the opportunity to share your thoughts with the consultant. If no such study is planned and you have the opportunity to propose one—do it.

The best avenue is developing the kind of rapport with your superior that will lead him or her to seek your advice and counsel. Remember—you're trying to convince the per-

son with the power to make changes; that a more comprehensive marketing group will be better for the agency, and
that you're *not* after a better position, increased power, or
more money (though these are nice byproducts).

Any of the avenues will take time. A more beneficial
structure begins with you recognizing that change is called
for, in order for you to deliver the best results for the agency
and the customer. From there it's all preparation, patience,
and perseverance, while putting maximum effort into your
daily performance.

The public sector could take a page from most any team
sport and think about a fresh start at least every couple of
years. Instead, there's an inertia to live with and perpetu-
ate an inappropriate structure and line up, even though
conditions and demands change. Personnel moves are risky
and unpopular in the security-conscious public sector. But
they're proper—if you're looking for the best results and
aren't afraid to rock the boat.

THE PLANNING PARTNER

In Figure 4 marketing and planning are listed together as
one top-level group in *a*. More and more public agencies,
and many in the private sector, are combining these forces
under a single head. They realize that the two must operate
as partners in shaping the service. The major peril is that a
planner with little appreciation or aptitude for marketing
may become head of the combined unit. That is much worse
than having separate marketing and planning groups reporting directly to the chief executive. With a marketer in
charge of a combined group, the marketing clout is maxi-
mized, assuming support from the top. However, that struc-

ture carries a corresponding responsibility for the marketer to become adept in planning management.

If the two are not consolidated into a major group, seek a close working relationship up and down the line with the planners because they have strong impact on service design. Research is the tie that binds the two groups together and is marketing's strong suit in the relationship.

THE MARKETING GROUP

Assuming the top-level structure is favorable—or something you can work on with hope of improvement—the next concern is organization of the marketing group itself. A proven, commonsense approach is to establish separate units for basic customer services and market-planning/promotional functions, including research. If you're fortunate to embrace all of the functions described in Chapter 1, then more units will be necessary, but the customer service and planning/promotion split will work in the majority of cases. A third logical unit is public relations, comprising any or all of the activities described in Chapter 1.

Be prepared for some feelings of inferiority from the customer–service unit. The services category is considered less glamorous, but it's the bread-and-butter of most businesses. Promotion is higher profile, by definition, and most perceive it as exciting (especially if you have the backing to do paid television). The same is true for public relations. The task here is to treat each unit with the same balanced consideration the good football coach gives the offensive, defensive, and special teams (or how a good chief executive treats the major organizational units). How you do that is up to you and your individual style. If you don't, dissension is guaranteed.

RESPONSIBILITY MATRIX
(for major publication)

Functions	LD	LC	ET	KB	DP	GF	DB	GH	BN
Contracts		A					P		
Advertising		A		P					
Consultant Coordination	A	P		S					
Type/Pasteup	P		A	S					
Stripper Coordination	P		A	S					
Printer Coordination	P		A	S					
Editorial/Copy	A				S	S		P	
Proofing	P		A	S	S	S			
Symbol Proof									P
Free-list Proof									P
Filler Copy		P			S	S			
Distribution Plan	A	P							

Responsibility Key: P-Primary; A-Advisory; S-Support

Figure 5. A matrix useful in assigning levels of responsibility, by task, for a project or program.

A common complaint from employees is: "I don't know what I'm supposed to do." There are a number of ways to end this frequently heard complaint. Take the time to sit down and write job descriptions for each position, if there are none. Rewrite them, if necessary. This is time well-spent because it describes the position and its responsibilities explicitly. The format is not nearly as important as the fact that you develop the descriptions in a consistent manner, taking great care to avoid overlaps in responsibility. And use it as a contract for measuring job performance.

If there are overlaps, these will surface when you develop a second helpful item—the responsibility matrix, as illustrated in Figure 5. It's more than that, really, since it sharply defines responsibilities and goes a long way toward defining authority, too. The matrix consists of the names (initials) of all those in the marketing group on one axis and a list of all of the functions the group performs on the other. In the blocks in the body of the matrix, mark a P for primary, an A for advisory, and an S for support responsibility as you match the people and functions. Leave it blank if they have no responsibility for a particular function. This is best to work through in a group setting because of the education that results for all concerned during the interchange. It's likely that your own views of your and other jobs will be modified during such a discussion.

The sorting out of responsibilities also begins to spell out authority in the respective functional areas. In simpler language, it identifies turf. Like propaganda, turf usually has a negative connotation, but the identification of turf—and tenacious defense of turf for the right reasons—is positive and productive.

As an example, in my early years with Metro Transit in Seattle, the production of more than 3 million complex timetables for more than 100 bus routes three times a year was a sizable headache. After suffering through many missed deadlines, errors, and conflicts among the four parties (three not in the marketing group) sharing responsibility for the product, I managed to get final responsibility placed squarely in the hands of the marketing person. The improvements in punctuality and quality were immediate. Ever afterward, I—and the subordinate responsible— were extremely protective of that turf for the right reasons; it ensured a better product and better service to the customer.

STAFF STRENGTH AND CONTROLS

After assessing staff structure and responsibilities, you're ready to review just how adequately staffed you are to deliver on expectations (at least the expectations as you understand them at this point—without the benefit of the annual marketing plan that will clarify staff needs more precisely). You also need the plan to help justify any requests for more staff.

As with the structure, you should still take a hard look at your staff situation in relation to what you perceive has to be done. Often the marketer is expected to be a one-person miracle worker with a list of duties that are obviously too much to tackle. In that situation, it's imperative to talk with your superior first, rather than try to take on more than you can handle and get deeper and deeper into trouble in the process. Once you're satisfied that you generally have the people to do what's expected, or your duties have been trimmed to fit, you can begin planning and refine the personnel needs later.

An obvious and common way to complement staff shortages is through the use of consultants, although employing them to do normal staff work is not their highest and best use. The preferred use is as on-call experts for short-term advice and support in the scientific areas of marketing (i.e., research design, market segmentation, forecasting, pricing, and media-buying). These are areas that require expertise too costly to keep on the permanent payroll when they're needed only intermittently. (More about consultants in Chapter 6.)

Controls over work flow are indispensable from the start. Whatever your methods and level of sophistication, develop a system you're comfortable with for keeping tabs on money, production deadlines, and performance. These can range from hand drawn "milestone" charts to the more exotic computer-generated program evaluation and review technique (PERT) charts for deadline tracking. You should also have some type of small sign off stamp to put on all production pieces requiring your or others' approval (initials). Budget and performance tracking, likewise, are done in a variety of ways. The important thing is to know the status of key indicators in all of these areas all of the time—or where to find the needed information in a hurry. Some managers establish such complex controls that the controls become an end in themselves, rather than a means to the end of better and more productive performance. Do it your way. But do it.

Computers are a godsend to the marketer, particularly when it comes to producing control sheets and dealing with the reams of research data and presentation requirements that result from the marketing process. Many people (marketers included) are either so intimidated or entranced by the computer that they fail to recognize its true utility. The computer is first and foremost the means for quickly storing, retrieving, and packaging infinite amounts of information that are too time-consuming, if not impossible, to do manually. Take a hands-on course and learn to operate one, by all means, if you haven't yet. Keep in mind that, as a marketer, you're most interested in learning and perfecting ways the computer can help you to analyze, package, and present information more rapidly and effectively to your colleagues and the public. Automated data processing (ADP) and management information systems (MIS) are basic to any bureaucracy in the computer age.

SPENDING AUTHORITY

Almost as sad as the outnumbered or understaffed marketer is the one who has to go through six different people just to get authority to buy a pack of pencils. The head (or lone) marketer, above all others, must have the ability to spend quickly within the limits of an authorized budget. Marketing needs are hard to anticipate in this fast-paced world of multimedia campaigns and other promotional activities where changes to take advantage of unforeseen opportunities (or for other reasons) are a fact of life.

Spending authority ranks below structure and staff resources as a priority. But if you can get your superior's O.K. on an adequate amount (somewhere between $1,000 and $5,000) that you can spend on one purchase order without going to higher authority, you'll be even better prepared to perform.

If your purchase order process is preordained and complicated (many steps), the only recourse is to practice communication and cooperation. A bit of the personal touch with the key people at each step of the sign off chain will do wonders to get fast action when you need it. You'll help your cause immensely if you save the "rush" orders for extreme emergencies and process the routine purchase orders with plenty of lead time.

KNOW THE GOALS

From basic details to grand direction—it's time for the last bit of preparation for the planning phase. Somewhere in your talks with your boss be sure to ask him or her about departmental goals (maybe even a grand goal) for the organization. And discuss whether he or she wants you to do a long-range plan (three to five years) initially, or focus first on the all-important annual marketing plan and do the long-range plan when you're finished (the preferred alternative).

Many agencies schedule a one- or two-day retreat at this point to discuss general direction, establish "goal congruence" (a fancy term for checking out where everybody's coming from), and discuss the planning process. You should suggest this if it's not scheduled. It's well worth the several hundred dollars that it will cost to get away from the office, and outside interruptions, in order to discuss these matters in an informal and relaxed setting with all members of the management team. The goal-congruence exercise can begin by choosing 8 to 10 personal values (e.g., security/career development, contribution to the community, recognition, teamwork, etc.) and seeing how much agreement—or disagreement—exists among team members in their relative ranking of these values. This is a most revealing and helpful starting point in formulating goals for the agency.

Management-by-objectives also is popular in public agencies. If you have such a program, it will ensure that you have a mission and goals statement and the framework for objectives that will evolve from your marketing planning effort. With the input from a top-level retreat, you can begin work with members of the marketing group and peers who will be counted on for key contributions and should be involved in objectives setting.

What a pleasure it is to prepare for your own planning phase with support and guidance from the top, a balance of strength with your peer groups, a staff that is adequate and knows its job, the controls in place, and the necessary spending authority. With these resources, you're poised to succeed. And best of all—the job will be more fun.

3

customer service

BUILD THE "LAUNCHING PAD"

Think of customer service like the launching pad for a space rocket. The marketing moon shot you're about to plan will never leave the ground without a solid base to spring from.   The rocket (promotion) is the glamour, but the launching pad (customer service) makes it all possible.

This doesn't mean that customer service should be passive and perfunctory. Just the opposite. It can and should be every bit as active and aggressive as the promotional effort. However, don't plan for a big promotional push unless the customer-service program is in good shape. And if it is, keep a close check on its status.

In many public agencies, customer service represents the majority of the marketing program. In fact, it's the basis for establishing a *marketing orientation,* which says the agency exists for the customer not the operators of the agency (an operations orientation).

The essential elements of customer service are telephone information, complaint-handling, some kind of walk-in center where customers can be served face to face, and basic printed information. There are many potential special services that can be added to this nucleus, but first the main elements.

TELEPHONE INFORMATION

Aided by the computer, telephone information is undergoing a transformation. However, many public-sector telephone services are handled in a manual mode with operators who provide information from printed or microfiche information sources. Stringent training is a must for most public-sector information operators. This is particularly true in something as complex as a large transit system. The length of the training period depends on how long it takes the trainee to reach the level of proficiency that you have set forth. Some will take less and others more time than the norm. Just be sure not to set a fixed course, put the trainees through it, and then consider them ready to tackle the telephones—ready or not.

In your training program you're going for a balance between quality and quantity (efficiency) in call handling. Based on your own particular service, determine standards for call length and the number of calls an operator should handle per hour, on averge. From there it's a matter of the operator having a thorough knowledge of the service area (if local) and the service you provide, along with up-to-the minute changes in any aspect of service. Never forget, nor let them forget, that this is the front line.

Many agencies have a monitoring system so that a supervisor can listen in to gauge the operator's performance in handling customer calls. This can be a sensitive issue, so it's important to explain to those affected why it's being done. Constructive feedback and praise for good performance—where warranted—help make the practice a positive experience.

Computer-based modules for telephone operators and clerks are coming to the public sector slowly but surely. They're a must in private-sector businesses like real-estate networks, travel agencies, and the airlines, who pioneered the use of computers for information and ticketing.

The transit industry probably represents the most complex and costly computerization challenge in the entire public sector. To begin with, the information input to the computer is massive and extremely detailed (many routes, multiple trip times), which requires huge capacity and sophisticated programming capabilities. Once the database is set, the operators are capable of giving only scheduled—rather than actual—bus times. Unfortunately, in systems of any size, buses often get delayed in traffic, which can invalidate some of the information being provided over the telephone.

Systems that are going to computer-based information deal with the dilemma by providing computer updates on delayed buses through the dispatcher's office. And there, two-way radios are being complemented in a few systems by computerized tracking networks that automatically monitor the on-time status of each bus in the system.

In the final and most sophisticated stage, transmitter units are installed on each bus to signal the precise location. Thus, a person can call a predetermined telephone number for a specific bus stop and a computer-generated voice will give the real-time arrival information for the next two buses due at that stop. The live operator is only required to intervene for more detailed inquiries, which is usually about half the calls.

Interestingly, this real-time information system is being introduced into the transit industry largely as a marketing tool. In several bus systems where it is operational in the United States and Canada, it appears to have a strong positive impact on peoples' confidence in the reliability of service—which translates into more riders. This is particularly true in the off-peak (noncommute) hours when buses generally run less frequently.

This lengthy discussion about the real-time information system for transit is significant. If the transit industry can adapt successfully to computer information, any public agency can. Virtually all other public services have static facilities and places of business, as compared with hundreds or thousands of buses running all over a service area most hours of the day. On the other hand, if your information requirements are so simple that the manual mode is still a good and economical way to provide the needed information, stick with it. Don't go to computers just to go to computers. They are a means to better service, where appropriate, and the end must justify the cost of conversion.

If your current manual system is clearly inadequate, then conversion to computer is justifiable on that basis alone. Recall the Chapter 1 example of demarketing where customers of a transit system were urged to shift from reliance on the telephone to other information aids. That was necessary because the system was inadequate. With a real-time system the tables would be turned and the telephone would become a strong marketing tool (which it really should be).

This raises the question as to how actively a public agency should get into the business of telephone marketing, popularly called telemarketing. This is where the operator takes the initiative to place the call, as well as receive inquiries. Some public agencies will have operators place calls about new services or products when they are not busy with in-coming calls, or add a bit of a sales-pitch at the end of an in-coming call. (The private sector is getting into telemarketing in a big way. Businesses recognize that face-to-face sales calls cost $150 to $200 each, as compared with only $15 to $20 per telephone call. Along with this is the time saved and the ability to reach more customers.) As a public agency, you should try telemarketing if you have the telephone capacity and time.

COMPLAINT HANDLING

The name of the game in the public sector still is responding to the public, and that includes handling complaints. If at all possible, separate complaints from information calls. Have separate telephone numbers and staffs because the nature of the work is distinctly different and requires different temperaments. In many cases, a single secretary has to do triple duty in providing information, taking complaints, and handling general calls. If the traffic is light, this is fine. It isn't acceptable though in a high-visibility agency with a heavy volume of information and complaint calls.

If you have a separate staff to handle complaint calls (as well as commendations), they must be up-to-the-minute on any known changes in the status of service, just as the information operators must be. Any level of computer assistance will, of course, facilitate these front liners in getting immediate word from the operations staff.

Instill complaint handlers with the idea that their ultimate value is in achieving solutions for problems identified via the complaint process. Too many complaint offices see themselves as the dead-end depository of endless gripes, and nothing more. This robs them of the feeling that they can do something about valid complaints, weakens the marketing orientation, and—worst of all—lessens service quality.

WALK-IN CENTERS

Walk-in centers should be situated for the convenience of your customers, not the agency. If you only have one center, it should be as close as possible to the core of your service area and take into account the ease of access for the disabled—both in reaching the center and moving about inside. Remember, too, the earlier comments about the importance of your public face. This is where it really shows.

Courteous and competent clerks are a prerequisite. From there it's up to their supervisor to ensure they have the tools and information to work with. If money handling is involved, security is a major consideration. Give it careful attention until you're fully satisfied that the system is secure and working well. Often the promotion people can forget to display copies of all of their materials at the walk-in center. Banners, buttons, and other specialty items help dress up the center and keep it part of the overall marketing effort. This sounds obvious, but you'd be surprised how often you can walk into such a center and not see or be able to get items the promotion people are distributing liberally—to others.

BASIC INFORMATION

A basic information piece, like a zoo guide or recruiting pamphlet, is part of the customer-service nucleus—not part of promotion. Virtually any agency or nonprofit association needs a brochure or tabloid that explains the service to any interested member of the public, whether a user of the service or a taxpayer who wants to know what his or her tax dollars are buying. This piece should be consistent with the promotional materials in tone, style, and appearance (color and graphics) and even carry the current promotional theme and supporting copy if possible.

Using the walk-in centers and basic brochure to complement promotions builds cohesiveness between the customer–service and promotion units and adds to the over-all impact of your marketing program. There also is a strong public relations aspect to customer service that can do much to enhance—or detract from—the agency's public image. Thus, the people dealing with the media must be kept abreast of customer-service activities and actions.

Inquiries from media organizations that run consumer

advocate columns or commentaries are a useful line of communication and should be handled with extreme care. Whether the responsibility is assigned to a customer service or public relations staffer, or someone else, it is important to provide rapid, thorough, accurate, and candid replies. It is possible, with this kind of response, to have the columnist or commentator render a positive (from your standpoint) report from investigation of the inquiry or complaint. Better yet, it's a good way to supply background on controversial issues that might go unheeded in another context. More than once, sensitive issues have been defused because the agency had an opportunity to explain the reasons and rationale for a particular action, in response to an inquiring reporter. Careful response—every time over a long period of time—is the secret to success.

SPECIAL SERVICES

There is a limitless list of special services that an agency can employ to better serve its customers. One of the most common of these is mobile customer–service vehicles of the type used, for example, by energy or telephone utilities. This kind of outreach demonstrates an active, rather than passive, approach to customer service. An agency that offers picture ID passes to elderly and disabled customers also might consider an ongoing program to visit homes for the elderly and disabled where they issue the passes with the aid of a portable camera. This also exemplifies a marketing rather than operations orientation.

The disabled community represents a real responsibility for public agencies. While the degree to which the commitment is carried out can be debated, the responsibility to provide information and access to service cannot. Transit systems are in the forefront of this issue because they touch so many people so often every day. Some of the steps taken by transit systems in behalf of the disabled include: facilities in telephone–information centers to receive and send typewritten messages to deaf callers equipped with a special telephone, lifts and tie-downs on buses to accommodate wheelchair passengers, and customized lift-equipped vans. Some systems even print timetables in braille.

Yet another transit special service is the staffing of a lost-and-found counter. Most agencies have dropped it because of the cost. Those that still offer the service reap generous good will for their troubles. This can be extended by donating the unclaimed items to charity. Even better, they can be auctioned off (good public relations opportunity) and the receipts given to charity. In case you wondered, the inventory of lost items can be bizarre—ranging from false teeth to small bags of marijuana, in the case of one big city system.

There's a tendency to get lulled into inattention to customer service because it's the more routine part of the marketing job—despite the added initiatives you may undertake. To avoid this, build a strong customer–service component into your management controls. At a minimum, you want to track telephone calls, complaints, and counter traffic.

In the telephone area, keep watch on the number of hourly and daily calls taken and lost, the average number of calls handled per operator per hour, and the average length of each call. Most telephone companies, for a price, offer automated equipment that will record these data.

Categorize complaints by major area (i.e., operations, planning, marketing, maintenance, etc.), and track by type, time of day, and point of origin in the service area. And most important, the control report should state the status of the fixes made or in progress.

Walk-in counter controls should cover the daily cash flow and numbers relating to sales or issuance of items dispensed through the center. In checking the customer–service controls as well as other controls, look for red flags (a sudden jump in lost calls or drop in cash revenue). The checks should be made biweekly or monthly, at the latest. (Feedback through these control sources is a form of research information and should be put into the data bank for use in planning and evaluation.)

All told, the number and quality of your customer–service offerings are a principal measure of your agency's marketing orientation and reflect the very quality of the agency itself.

A MARKETING ORIENTATION

The challenge of infusing a public agency with a marketing orientation is a marketer's highest calling. Few get the opportunity to begin on a positive footing because it's easier to avoid rather than accommodate the public. Usually the marketer is faced with achieving conversion from an operations orientation dictated by old-line operators or leaders who place emphasis on operating activities.

The transit industry is not too long removed from the days when the company was satisfied if all the buses ran on time—whether there was anyone there to ride them or not. The comedy sketches about bus drivers pulling off and shutting the door in the face of a person running to board were more fact than fiction.

I fought a classic marketing versus operations battle early in my transit career. The bus system operated a route southbound into downtown and the same bus continued through downtown and on south as another route. The first route was, let's say, 43 and the second 29. It had long been the practice for the driver to only change the roller sign above the front windows at the ends of each route, during lay-over time, because it was more convenient and saved time and hassle.

The trouble was the customer suffered. When the 43 was headed for downtown the sign was O.K. But as the bus continued through, those waiting in downtown were looking for the 29, not the 43, as the sign read. Same thing going back in the other direction, only it was 29 all the way.

At the time there were a half dozen pairs of routes like these and as the system grew there were more than a dozen. Amazingly, the customers adapted. When the agency began installing new bus stops with the route numbers boldly displayed, I finally won the long battle to have the drivers change their roller signs at the edge of downtown so that the route number on the bus matched the one the customer was looking for. Hard to believe—but true. In the not-too-distant past, this kind of cavalier disregard for the customer was commonplace in many public agencies.

On an individual level, a marketing orientation means that each person in the organization puts himself or herself in the customer's place in every contact and seeks to help— no matter how seemingly stupid or openly hostile the question. Unfortunately, the more common condition is to be so concerned with paperwork or personal matters that the customer is considered an intrusion. This is more true in the public bureaucracy than in the less-secure, profit-driven private sector.

Once more, the chief executive is pivotal in creating the kind of climate that puts the customer first. But everyone, from top to bottom, should put every interaction to the test of whether it's being done more for the convenience of the agency or the customer. On a day to day basis be responsive—not resistant—where the customer is concerned.

As a philosophy, tell the public what they can do, not what they can't do. I'm reminded of a sign I saw once on a fence at a nearby school athletic field. It said: "No use of this field without prior administrative approval—RCW 98-28-107." It should have said something like: "For approval to use this field, please call 555-6879." Guess which one conveys the marketing orientation?

You can't develop a marketing orientation in a vacuum or will it into being overnight. It's not a marketing project; it's a feeling of genuine concern for the customer, developed over time, that infects all in the organization. Communication, cooperation, perseverance are the means. It's a never-ending job to get everyone caring personally about service quality, empathizing with the customer, and feeling that he or she is contributing personally to the success of the service and is responsible for everything that happens.

A marketing orientation is more than just so many words. It is the hallmark of the highest rated public agencies and top Fortune 500 corporations alike. You should ask yourself the following question: Is our marketing orientation suffering at the hands of the operations types and others, or gaining strength every day?

Chances are you're closer to the latter situation. An operations orientation is death these days. Television has transformed an apathetic public into one more aware and involved in the world around them, making a customer-be-damned attitude impossible in the public sector today. Consumerism is alive and growing and must be respected. This can only aid your cause.

If you feel the launching pad is solid, it's time to begin preparing for your marketing moon shot—with research.

4

---

research

USE THE RESULTS

If you aren't doing—and using—research, you aren't doing marketing. It's as simple as that. Research is to marketing as the senses are to the human body: Inseparable, inherent, and indispensable.

Research is the core of the marketing science. Identifying, analyzing, and measuring public and customer behavior demand a special expertise. Your job is to know the research requirements, understand how and when to employ them, and use the results properly in promoting your service to the public you're seeking to attract as customers—or at least supporters.

It's almost axiomatic that you can use consultants for all three phases of the marketing process: in the planning phase to accomplish those parts of the situation analysis that require quantitative and qualitative measures; in the promotional phase to test media concepts, themes, and new products; and in the evaluation phase to help assess results of the promotional efforts and the new attitudes toward your service.

It's easy to become so immersed in data and research options that you get bogged down and don't keep your eye on the overall aim of using research to get results. If you're just beginning, take a basic approach the first year and get better each year afterward. Research-based planning, like promotion and evaluation, all take time to perfect—if, indeed, perfection is possible.

ABOUT SAMPLING

Virtually all of the research methods you will employ involve sampling—a scientific process for deriving data from a small portion of the population you are surveying that can be projected to the entire population in the survey universe. Names of potential respondents usually are drawn from telephone books or reverse directories. Professional survey firms know how to do this best in your area. Sampling is least expensive when you can match your survey boundaries to well-defined areas, such as census tracts and zip code or telephone-prefix blocks.

The number of sampling cases (individual responses) is related to the level of confidence you want to achieve, not the size of the population being surveyed. A minimum of 400 cases and a confidence level of plus/minus 5 percent is standard for most telephone or interview surveys. Close issues—such as an election measure that is running near 50–50 in early polling—require more cases. And if market segmentation is involved, at least 1000 cases are desirable.

THE MAIN METHODS

The research methods described in the following are the main shopping list, but by no means all of the research resources at your disposal. However, with these (and assistance) you can carry out any public-sector marketing assignment in a competent manner. Look to these first and add sophistication as your program matures.

Always begin any research effort with a thorough check of the secondary sources listed in the Glossary, as well as prior studies by your own agency. Secondary research is existing information appropriate to your particular needs. Primary research is gathering nonexistent data from the public at large. In some instances you may not need primary research at all. But anytime the situation calls for public or consumer opinions, primary research initiated by you becomes necessary. It also may be possible to piggyback on a study by another public or private group for a nominal share of the cost.

Of the primary methods, personal interviews and telephone surveys are the most widely used for gathering initial and follow-up data. At a cost of $25 to $50 an interview (compared with $5 to $10 for telephone), personal interviews are almost always too expensive for all but the best-funded agencies or group of agencies. And either personal or telephone surveys are not cost effective for small (neighborhood level) geographic areas.

The strengths of the personal interview, which is most often conducted in the home, are the ability to probe in-depth and to ask more questions than is usually possible with a telephone survey.

Telephone research is faster and less expensive than personal interviews but is meeting some resistance from those who view it as an invasion of privacy. The computer-generated telephone voice that sounds like someone straight out of Orwell's *1984* doesn't help matters. Several concerned research houses even have placed advertisements in the print media to explain the importance of responding to telephone surveys. They contend that if their clients know what the consumers want they'll be able to reduce their range of product offerings and, in turn, cut the prices of those they produce. For the public sector the same kind of appeal can be made on the basis of being able to tailor services more appropriately and thus make them more economical.

Mail questionnaires are perhaps the most popular because good information can be gained at relatively low cost, assuming a good rate of return (30 percent or more of those mailed). Mailing lists are available for purchase from list houses, either by name or address only (occupant lists), or they can be obtained from telephone books, reverse directories, or other sources like professional associations. Census tract maps, available from the Bureau of the Census for a small fee, are valuable in preparing your mailing. The supplier lists are provided by census tract. List suppliers also can give you good information on postal regulations and rates.

Fundamental concerns relating to the confidence level of all research are the quality of the sample and questions that have been drawn, and the effect of both on the validity (does it measure what it purports to measure) and reliability (would it measure the same thing consistently) of the study. This is where expertise is essential because it's relatively easy to introduce bias into a study at virtually any point. With hundreds of thousands or even millions of dollars riding on guidance from research results, this is no place for novices. Your job is not to *do* the research but to judge its worth and apply it.

Intercept interviews, conducted by an interviewer on the street, are a quick-and-dirty (and inexpensive) way of getting information about an issue or sample product. These are rapid (maximum six questions) contacts made with people who come by a particular point or done in a roving-reporter manner. The quality of these results cannot begin to compare with even a mail questionnaire because of the unscientific sampling approach.

Another form of mail surveying is the postcard survey, which suffers from the same kind of confidence problems as the intercept interview. (However, both are better than the newspaper coupon or radio/television call-in surveys, which are the least valid and reliable of all recognized techniques.) Two other points about the postcard: if it's used (offered as a "take one") in places frequented only by customers of the surveyed product, you miss the whole noncustomer population, and this leaves you with no information on the potential market. Also, those most favorable are more likely to respond.

Focus groups, cross-sectional groups of 8 to 10 people led by a facilitator, are best used in pretesting research questionnaires, media-campaign concepts, and new products, like maps or packaging designs. These are considered a qualitative technique because they yield personal impressions instead of numerical ratings like the quantitative techniques of personal interviews, telephone surveys, and mail questionnaires. Focus groups tell you what some people may think, not what all people do think. They are helpful in getting a range of opinion prior to more representative survey research.

The facilitator is critical to the focus-group process. A good one doesn't lead the group to a conclusion but keeps discussion flowing in a desired direction. The result after several of these sessions with cross sections of several market segments is a solid feel for how a particular concept or product will be received. The results from these sessions shouldn't be the sole basis on which you make a decision to go or stop on a project, but they provide invaluable insight. Most research houses have a viewing room with a one-way mirror looking into the conference room. This allows the client to watch the focus groups in progress and to hear the comments first-hand, rather than having to rely solely on a written report or sit in the meeting and inhibit the discussion. You also may want to videotape the session (with the participants' permission). This enables you to review the discussion and to show it to others who might be interested.

This method is relatively inexpensive. The cost varies with the number of sessions you conduct and whether you pay the participants and how much. (These costs are in the research contract.) Something in the range of $10 to $20 a meeting, with some refreshments like sandwiches, cookies, coffee, and soft drinks thrown in, are helpful enticements to full participation. Too many no-shows (you need at least six people) can invalidate the discussion (it's easier for one individual to dominate and the perspective is too narrow) and that means costly rescheduling and delays.

Recognition and recall testing is a follow-up technique to measure the relative impact (awareness) achieved with a particular promotional campaign. These can be either quantitative or qualitative—or a combination of the two (e.g., telephone survey and diary). The combination is preferable, because these results are vital to the evaluation of your promotional efforts.

In the computer age, the science of primary research is more sophisticated than ever. Many of the new methodologies and simulation modeling techniques are discussed in detail in books under the research heading in the Reference section. Unless you decide to specialize in research, read for a general understanding of what the respective tools can contribute so that you can call on experts to employ them if needed sometime in the future.

READABLE REPORTS

For all of their expertise, many research firms have a real inability to reduce data into intelligible information and reports that can be readily applied to specific needs. All too frequently the final study reports are a mass of data and hard-to-read tables. If you picture yourself holding from $5,000 to $50,000 in cash (the cost range of research studies) in your hands as you try to fathom such a report, you get a better appreciation for the seriousness of the subject.

It's not fair, however, to blame the consultant completely. The marketer (client) has a distinct responsibility to outline the study objectives in detail at the outset, before any other work is begun. The importance of close communication between the client and researcher can't be overemphasized. This kind of collaboration is especially important when the client intends to act immediately on the researcher's findings. A good technique is to establish a framework for the formatting of those findings that fits the annual marketing plan format. Here's one that works well:

1. The awareness of and attitudes toward present service

2. The profile of present and potential market segments, their behavior, and level of demand

3. The messages that are most effective with the current and prospective segments and the best media to reach them (including recognition and recall of previous promotions)

4. The results from special questions (e.g., response to a proposed fee increase/new product, etc.)

This breakdown basically tells you what people think about your present service, who's using it, who the prospective users are, and how to reach them. It's a simplified and logical approach guaranteed to aid in the comprehension of any research-study report. Put the researchers on notice, too, that you expect some nice simple bar charts and pie charts to help communicate the findings even more clearly. They're a snap with computers.

Though you want and need simplicity in results, don't demand it in the analysis. This is what creates those reams of near-useless banner tables comparing only two variables at a time. You can't understand a "multivariate" world through masses of two-way relationships. A good researcher will first interrelate similar measures, then go through a data-reduction step that creates indices to represent key concepts. Then he or she will use multivariate methods to predict the important measurement criteria. Finally, the researcher will produce tables and charts using those measures that are strongest in predicting each criterion.

With the objectives and reporting framework mutually understood, you have a head start on receiving a useful report down the road and are ready to begin development of the all-important questionnaire. Don't come near the point of writing questions, for the reasons mentioned earlier. This is also what you're paying the experts for. However, do get more specific about what you want to know in relation to the objectives and four-part reporting format. And be sure to tell the researcher in the study-design stage your range of possible actions in relation to the subject being studied. Knowing this, the researcher can design questions that produce the most relevant information on which to base decisions.

Remember the value of keeping a solid base of tracking questions if this is the successor to a similar study or studies. Two tips to keep in mind are: (1) try to retain at least two-thirds of the questions from before (assuming they covered all major areas of interest in the four-part format) and (2) keep these "baseline" questions as nearly the same as possible. While the results from one study are valuable, the value increases exponentially as years of tracking data are laid on one another—even if it merely shows that nothing much has changed. This is solid information and perspective that will be invaluable in your planning work.

Armed with your input, it is fairly routine work for the trained researcher to perfect old questions or develop new ones to elicit the required information. The most predictable problem you'll encounter is holding the questionnaire to a reasonable length. Everyone always wants to ask more questions than researchers recommend in order to get good cooperation and responses from those interviewed or called. The maximum length for a telephone interview is about 15 minutes, with eight being preferable. Personal interviews probably should not exceed two pages.

The types of questions and the mix are part of the researcher's art. The most common kinds are closed-end, forced-choice, and open-end, all defined in the Glossary. The type of question chosen to elicit a response has much to do with the quality of the response and, in turn, the survey itself.

A standard quantitative survey takes nearly three months from start to final report. This includes about two weeks for field work (calling or interviewing), one week for coding and entering data, four weeks for analyzing the results, and two weeks for writing and preparation of the final report.

USING THE RESULTS

With this kind of investment of public tax dollars, it's imperative that you use the results. And it's important to understand what using the results means.

Some people (often chief executives, unfortunately) think research should tell you what to do. It won't, or shouldn't, as such. Research can only give you a perspective on important pieces of the total picture you will endeavor to develop in doing the situation analysis of your annual plan. Beyond that it is usually a snapshot of conditions at a point in time and conditions can change rapidly. (Cross-time studies are more helpful if you can use and afford them.) And, any study, if not done carefully, can be misleading.

But assuming the best, the results should be used in a context that considers all other factors impacting the situation, or at least those that are apparent and applicable. This is the role of the situation analysis and why it must be a comprehensive and logical document, leading to certain conclusions that provide the answers many expect research alone to provide.

Getting your full money's worth out of completed research begins with the final report. It should open with an executive summary so the reader can gain a quick overview of the findings (but with the caveat that he or she not jump to any conclusions). If the body is organized in those four categories and complemented with good charts, you're now in excellent shape to *use* the research. Now you should:

- Distribute copies to your superior, key peers, and subordinates who will have major responsibilities in developing the annual marketing plan. (This assumes you involved the key players in the study-design stage.)
- Read and reread it several times and begin developing a list of other types of cross-tabulations you may be interested in.
- Look for insights that may be hidden in the data that your researchers overlooked. You, not they, are the expert in your particular situation.
- Think about even better ways to portray the information and identify information that should be in some kind of chart form, but isn't.

    (*Note:* You can add substantially to the report's value by putting as much of the data as possible in a comparative context. In working with the researcher on the tracking questions from previous similar studies (say the last three years), request that the report compare data for each of the four years side by side, insofar as possible. (This assumes you're in the tracking-study mode and that the prior data were derived from similar methods, sampling techniques, and questions.))

* Extract pages and charts from the report for use in a verbal presentation to the board, peer groups in the agency, your own group, or any other interested parties (like a professional association).

* And—most important—begin identifying follow-on research that may be required to satisfy the needs of the situation analysis process (more about that in Chapter 5).

DON'T LOOK FOR ANSWERS

In sum, to *use* research it has to be in understandable form and then employed in a context where it can help contribute to some conclusions. Whether its an extensive or limited effort, look for guidance and perspective out of research, not final answers. Answers are *your* responsibility and where your judgment is required after studying all of the information that has been amassed and analyzed.

A parting tip on dealing with researchers: Most have a tendency to want to "massage" the data far beyond deadlines. One of the main reasons much research is unused is that it was too late to make its way into the analytical process or product-development cycle. You simply can't go ahead without the research and leave what you've paid good public money for to come along later in its perfected form—after the fact. Do whatever it takes to make sure that doesn't happen.

With your marketing senses now functioning fully through research, you can begin the first major phase of the marketing process—planning.

5

planning

PREVENT "BRUSH FIRES"

"Brush fires" can burn you. The periodic—or constant—work crisis is a sure sign of poor planning up front.

Some employees are brush-fire bugs because they give one the appearance of being busy and engaged in important work. What the fire fighters really are doing is running double—or triple—time to do things they should have done days, weeks, or even months ago.

The real pain from brush fires is the disruptive effect on the whole rhythm and flow of the work pattern. There will always be the unforeseen situations that you must deal with in the midst of regular work. But you can prevent the recurring crises by planning in sufficient detail and communicating and coordinating your plans carefully with others.

Marketing planning, by definition, is the systematic reduction of all factors affecting your situation into an organized method of decision-making, implementation of decisions, and evaluation of results. This kind of orderly process is the marketer's best means of influencing the internal and external forces in a positive direction.

THE THREE PLANS

As a marketer you must be far-sighted—as well as myopic enough to keep an eye on immediate details. There are devices to help you deal in both the short and long range—and the period in between as well. They are the long-range plan, the project plan, and the fulcrum for both—the annual marketing plan.

Besides the overview and order these plans provide, there are some less-appreciated values, particularly with the annual plan. Just being involved in the plan-development process imprints it indelibly in your and your staff's minds so the instinctive and reflexive action you're seeking day to day is aided and abetted. The plans are definite decision-making tools. Sometimes you don't even recognize them as such. (If there's a dilemma between two priorities and one has to do with an objective in the annual plan, you'll choose that one.) The plans are controlling mechanisms, too, in the best sense of the word. They chart the course for your peers and even your superior to follow, assuming you've taken care to get their buy-off. Finally, the plans are excellent resource documents with value in direct proportion to the work you put into them. The situation analysis of the annual plan is particularly helpful in providing a summary of the background and status of the agency.

THE PLANNING MENTALITY

Do the plans right—and carefully—and they will pay large dividends in the long run. Planning, in fact, can be fun. Developing a planning mentality takes some effort and practice. One useful mental game (and it's much easier to employ on a three-month project than a long-range plan) is to picture in your mind the results you want when the project or plan reaches its climax.

The easiest and best illustration is a political campaign (a challenge virtually identical to marketing a public agency though more intense and final). Picture yourself as the campaign manager. At the outset of the campaign, well before the structure and strategies have been determined, you visualize exactly what you'd like to see and hear the weekend before the election (which is most often on a Tuesday). Picture yourself driving along, seeing dozens of yard signs, hearing your spot on the car radio, passing a couple of billboards, and then stopping to eat and picking up the newspaper to see a favorable editorial on your issue in one section and a full-page ad in the other (with copy matching that in the mailer now arriving at thousands of targeted households). And, finally, glancing up at the television above the counter to see your spot playing. And all are consistent in color, design, and message content.

As fantasy-like as it may sound, this kind of synergism and strength is possible to approximate—if you get the picture in your mind's eye and work from day one toward that ideal. One of the reasons that planning is either lip-serviced or done poorly is that most people seem to have an aversion to sitting and concentrating on something that's going to happen three to six months or a year later.

In the absence of a plan, and adherance to successive deadlines, you've lost precious lead time. Now you're left to regain those lost days by doing double- or triple-time—fighting brush fires—to the disservice of all concerned. Good planning is the preventative measure.

The annual plan is the centerpiece—between the long-range plan and project plans. (Outlines and descriptions of the elements of the annual/long-range plans and project plan are provided in Appendices B and C.) For each plan there are guidelines to be applied—as appropriate—to your situation. No two plans will be the same. The discipline of doing a plan is what counts, and each succeeding one will (should) get better. The place to begin is with the annual plan, unless your superior has directed you to do a long-range plan first.

The marketing-planning process is a rigorous exercise demanding consideration of all relevant information in a logical sequence. Deciding what information is relevant is a highly subjective matter and one that you will get better at with each succeeding plan. Much of the strength and credibility of the plan comes from the interactive process, which requires reiterating your work on individual sections and subsections to recheck their internal consistency and inter-related impacts. The other key is competent work on the individual elements, which include: executive summary, mission and goals, situation analysis, objectives and strategies, promotional program, and evaluation.

Even though the executive summary comes first, it's the last thing you should prepare after the other parts of the plan are completed. Since it's the only thing that many may read in your plan, make it concise, compelling, and convincing. Next up-front are the mission and goals. A classic mission statement is the Strategic Air Command's "Peace Is Our Profession"–the very model of brevity and clarity. Many mission statements are often long winded; the definition of mission is lost in words and with it the chance to motivate employees through a clear sense of purpose. Hopefully, you and your staff have been fully involved in drafting the mission statement, as well as your goals. If not, invent some and sell them to your superior and peers as a first step in getting them involved in the plan.

There's a distinct difference between goals and objectives, which too often are used as synonyms for each other. It's important to recognize the difference. Goals are where you want to be in several years. Objectives are things you can achieve in a given year that build toward the goals. Goals can be measurable; objectives *must* be measurable.

A former boss provided a prime example of a "grand goal" and achieved two other important ends at the same time. He said simply that our grand goal three years hence was to carry 57 million passengers on the Metro bus system. We then set annual objectives to move from the beginning level of 45 million to the 57 million annual passengers between the first and third years. We surpassed it in two.

Because of the clarity of the goal, he galvanized the staff into concerted action and achieved a strong marketing orientation all at the same time. In those two years, we had only three or four objectives each year in pursuit of that single goal. It confirmed that fewer is better when it comes to both the goals and objectives of any agency.

In approaching the body of the annual plan, think of it as an hourglass, which funnels the many particles of sand down through the narrow passage where they are redistributed below. Your sand is the myriad bits of data, which you sift and narrow to a point where you can draw conclusions and set objectives and then redistribute as strategies and programs for implementation throughout the year.

THE SITUATION ANALYSIS

The sifting process in planning is the situation analysis. This section, especially, will vary to suit your needs and circumstances. That's expected. Just take great care to make your analysis comprehensive and logical and to incorporate the best available research data and other pertinent information. Begin by enlisting the aid of your peers in finance and planning, particularly, because the well-done situation analysis will get into data and disciplines that will require their assistance. This also goes a long way toward establishing meaningful communication and ensuring cooperation later on during plan implementation.

Background

The sequence suggested in Appendix B begins with a broad look at the background—today and a year or two ahead. The first logical element is a full description of the service you offer, followed by a detailed review of the operating environment. Your service area is the marketplace and should be analyzed in terms of population, households, income, and any other parameters that help give you and others a feel for the area. The major markets can be identified generally here (school-aged youths, commuters, housewives, etc.) because they will be described in more detail when you get into market segmentation later on.

Then look in-depth at economic, political/governmental, social, and technological factors affecting your operating environment today, or in the near future. For example, if a recent change in political leadership in your service area resulted in a reshuffling of your policy board, this should be taken into account and evaluated. As a general rule, the narrative throughout the situation analysis should be as informative and complete as possible, yet concise and conclusive. You would explain—in this case—the previous board makeup, the action that occurred, the new makeup, and the implications of the change. You want to be as candid as possible throughout the plan. But since your plan is a public document, it may be the better part of valor to leave some things unsaid, as long as they're understood by those involved in implementing the plan (e.g., don't state that you expect the new board to be "antimarketing." If it's true, stress the need for stepped-up board contact and information.).

The competitive environment is seldom of the same intensity as in the private sector, yet it's still necessary to consider. For instance, a new, privately owned water-slide park built near one of several public parks you are responsible for marketing is competition and should be evaluated for its potential impact on the park's attendance. That's direct competition. Most of the public-sector agencies face indirect competition because they are providing the kinds of services to which there are several alternatives—with the notable exceptions of police and fire protection and electrical energy. The aim here, as in each step of the analysis, is to determine if there is activity of any kind that will impact your situation positively or negatively in the near future.

The review of organizational resources gets back to the basics of organization discussed in Chapter 2. For both the agency as a whole and the marketing group, you should consider the structure, staffing, and financial resources. Here's the place to begin addressing your concerns about structure and staffing (if you have them). If the problems are great, use discretion. Best take them up with the boss, directly, rather than hanging your frustrations out for all to see in a widely distributed document. The inclusion of an organizational chart is most helpful and useful. This is also the place to include the agency's long-range budget (the equivalent of a private-sector business plan) and to indicate the anticipated marketing-budget figure, if it's known. (This is with the recognition that you may want to go to the boss or board for an adjustment after your planning is completed.)

Performance

From this background overview, the analysis moves to performance. Data for up to five years of use of your service (enrollment, membership, recruits, ridership, etc.) is desirable, and the more detailed the better. The finer the breakdown you can provide (user characteristics, frequencies, etc.) the more useful it will be in developing the profiles and behavior of your key market segments.

If you organized your research report in the four-part

format suggested in Chapter 4, you can plug it in right here, beginning with awareness of your service and attitudes toward it. This is where you get the first objective assessment of whether you have lots of work to do on the service (product) or can begin with a medium to high promotional profile right away. If you're still awaiting the research results or can't afford this kind of primary research just yet, make some educated guesses based on secondary sources. And these can include newspaper clippings, customer comments, and information from your telephone and complaint opertors. (The latter two should be used in your analysis in any event.)

Market segmentation is the very crux of your analysis. In simple terms, you are breaking your total potential market into smaller parts with identifiable similarities. Most often these segments are described in demographic (age, income, occupation, living arrangement), geographic (location), psychographic (personal values), and use or nonuse of service terms.

Obviously, people will fall into one or several of these segments. The aim is to identify the segment or combination of segments that offer the largest potential return in use of your service, considering all of your other analysis information. Hence, the segments you select may not be the largest in terms of total size. This results in a description or profile of the group or groups you're seeking to target.

The market matrix shown in Figure 6 is made up of cubicles that each represent a segment of the total market. It is a copy of the three-dimensional matrix developed to analyze potential customers in the early years of the volunteer army. The percentage of American males in each age category was available through census (secondary) data. Primary research picked up at the point of determining

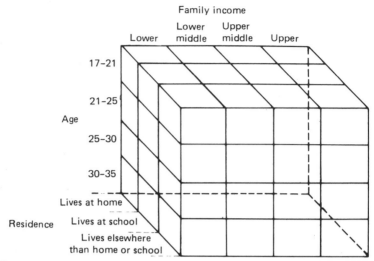

Figure 6. A market matrix showing potential groups of customers for the volunteer army (Reprinted with permission of Macmillan Publishing Co. from *Marketing* by James L. Heskett. Copyright © 1976 by James L. Heskett).

their family income, residence, and—most important—perceived needs and values. In the actual army marketing campaign, the army picked the age of 17 to 21, lower-middle income, lives-at-home profile as the target. They developed their advertising in response to the high value this group placed on a good place to work, learn, and enjoy themselves. The research presumably also was useful in going back and reworking the basic product offering, such as assignment preferences.

The real purpose of segmentation is to enable you to target your promotions. In the volunteer army example, the military had a budget of $26.7 million to promote its product to some 31 million males age 17 to 35, or only about 86 cents each. And this was not counting eligible females, those nearing age 17, and parents supportive of a military career for their children. With the cost of recruitment at about $1,000 per recruit, it was essential for the promotion to target and attract those who could pass muster and in sufficient numbers. It did. That's what good segmentation can deliver.

Behavior of the markets has to do with frequency of use, times of use, and related factors and is fairly simple to determine through quantitative research. Demand, in the public sector, is more difficult to assess but also is derived from quantitative research. There is less direct competition and the life-cycle of most services is in the mature stage, with only some occasional new products to stir demand.

Identifying effective messages is less exacting than segmentation but every bit as critical. Researchers typically identify various benefits and barriers to use of the service. They ask respondents their opinions on a scale from "very important" to "unimportant" or "no opinion." The responses are cross-tabulated against the demographics of the respondents and the messages that are appropriate to various segments begin surfacing.

I once managed a campaign to gain public approval of a sales-tax increase that provides a striking example of melding market segmentation and message in a winning way. In the first referendum, a general approach (appeal) failed by a narrow margin. In preparing for a repeat election on the issue two months later, my staff identified a well-defined lower-income area that they felt might increase its support with a clear statement of the direct benefits and "pennies-a-day" cost of the higher tax, in return for those benefits. They also felt that the other areas would, at least, maintain their previous level of support. With targeted delivery, this is precisely what happened and the tax increase passed.

The targeted delivery included door-to-door distribution
of the campaign brochure to communicate our message in
the chosen area in the 10 days just prior to the second
election. This was reinforced with yard signs and coffee
hours at homes of known supporters in the target area. The
whole experience also exemplified marketing action at its
best: getting the right service (in this case a service message) to the right market at the right price by the right
means at the right time.

The most-effective media and "other" sections of your
research format are relatively easy to elicit from interview
respondents. As indicated in Chapter 4, results from any
posttesting of previous promotions belongs here as well.

If you're just beginning the whole marketing process, you
may be doing your research study at the same time you're
working on other parts of the situation analysis so that it's
difficult to do things in sequence. The important thing is to
begin work on all the parts and worry about getting them
in sync later. (More about scheduling the process in Chapter 8.)

Pricing is definitely part of the science of marketing. If
you don't go to an outside consultant, you need someone on
staff with expertise in this arcane but all-important area.
Computer software packages are available to assist knowledgeable analysts in determining the best pricing structure, or at least in laying out the alternatives. One of the
primary things you will need to determine are the elastici-
ties (propensities to buy at various pricing levels) for the
various market segments that you have identified. In the
fourth part of your research format always include a couple
of questions to gauge how people feel about the current
pricing structure as a continuing in-road into the pricing
discussions.

Potential

Having sifted the background and performance data thoroughly, you're prepared for the most creative part of the analytical exercise—assessing the potential for increased use of your service through forecasting, seeking innovative ideas, and positioning (or repositioning) your service to enhance that potential.

In the public sector, the most common way of assessing potential is through questions in your baseline survey, combined with analysis of usage data from present and previous years. This should suffice for analysis purposes because the public sector largely moves along on its own inertia in the absence of the constant and direct competition that keeps the private sector ever-alert for new growth opportunities in order to survive.

Forecasting is a mixture of science and art that will require a collaborative effort with your peers in planning and finance, and possibly other groups, particularly if you expect the results to gain complete acceptance. Here's a good place to employ the delphi technique. (It can work well with pricing, too). It involves giving three or four people the data you've developed and asking them to render independent opinions on their forecasts of future sales. You then integrate the responses—in a process that may take several rounds—and reach a conclusion. Often, the forecasts have been made for you. In which case, you should lay those forecasts against the data you've developed and either accept them or take issue if you strongly disagree. Forecasting will be revisited in Chapter 6 in discussing the long-range plan.

Forecasting is serious business in all marketing—not just the private sector. The Washington State Lottery Commission was forced to undertake sudden and massive staff cuts soon after its inception when the sale of lottery tickets fell far short of projections. And the World's Fair in New Orleans made headlines with its multimillion dollar budget shortfall from failing to attract anywhere near the number of patrons it had predicted. If you're playing for these kind of stakes especially, do everything possible to get expert advice in forecasting.

Innovation should be on your mind throughout the planning process. A succession of solid innovations over time are the hallmark of progressive agencies and provide wide and positive public notice. They don't just happen; innovations emerge from a conscious and continuing effort to find new and better ways to serve the public.

Metro Transit's rise to recognition as the nation's best bus system in the mid-1980s would not have been possible without innovation: things like establishing the first free-ride area in downtown; introducing European articulated (bending) buses to America; and beginning an unprecedented program to get employers to subsidize all or part of the cost of a monthly bus pass. The last idea also afforded strong private-sector participation and led to other public-private cooperative projects. Private participation, in effect, represents another source of subsidy for public agencies and reduces the requirement for tax dollars or funds programs that might not otherwise be possible.

Figure 7 is promotional artwork for an innovative private-sector program aimed at helping public-transit systems generate added revenue and riders. Dubbed "Busgo," the on-board take-off on Bingo offers riders a variety of cash and merchandise prizes for matching numbers posted in the bus each week with those on playing cards distributed by the bus drivers.

Innovation and hard-hitting promotion are the key in-

Figure 7. A sample advertisement for Busgo (Reproduced with permission of AdPro).

gredients of an aggressive marketing program. They signal the fact that you're active and in control of your own destiny rather than passive and controlled by the influences that impact you almost daily. In the absence of a plan and a commitment to persevere on that plan, you are doomed to a defensive—and ultimately defeatist—posture. Strong stuff—but true.

POSITIONING

Good positioning is the closest thing to a quick-fix that marketing has to offer. Positioning, in plain terms, is describing your product to the target markets in a way that defines your own best attributes and, if possible, the shortcomings of the competition.

To do good positioning you must know your service thoroughly, study the available research, and figure on how to state its strengths to your best advantage, whether or not this means naming the competition. Some examples are provided in Chapter 6 in the discussion about themes, which—if not the same—are closely related.

Positioning that names and "defines" the competition is becoming more and more popular, particularly in the private sector and political campaigning. In a memorable Washington State gubernatorial race, the more experienced Republican candidate for the vacant governor's seat finished far behind the winning Democrat in the primary election. At the start of the general election run-off between the two, the Republican candidate came out with a position (theme) that declared: "Spellman is the Answer. McDermott is the Question." The new position was supported by a strong and cohesive multimedia campaign that incorporated the new theme in all of its elements and emphasized McDermott's inexperience. Spellman quickly closed the gap and won by a comfortable margin.

Positioning also can turn potential negatives into positives. In a Metro Transit project, my assignment was to plan for the change—literally overnight—of all the Metro bus-route names and numbers. With a service area of a million people and 1000 buses—the chance for public confusion and consternation was great. The name (position) we gave the project had much to do with its success. Instead of announcing that we were going to "change all the numbers and names of bus routes," we announced the "New Look" program—hitting hard on the benefits and lightly on the temporary confusion that might result. Needless to say, our customer-service staff was well-prepared for the transition—and the kudos far outnumbered the complaints.

This example also illustrates the fact that positioning applies to individual projects or products as well as your overall service. If you've done a solid job of market segmentation and have or plan to develop products specifically for these markets, then the positioning of each product should be reviewed in relation to each target market, for maximum effect. If you're doing a mailer to three very different segments in your service area, a shift in emphasis to better address each of their respective interests is bound to be more effective.

Positioning, too, is a mix of science and art. There are specialists available to assist you with the scientific aspects, if needed. Lots can be achieved just with common sense and creativity, using the information and analysis developed to this point. Whatever you do, don't overlook the power and promise of positioning in advancing your cause rapidly.

After considering possible innovations and new positioning, you will want to review your forecasts once more, recognizing that you still have to develop marketing strategies and projects that may increase the potential gains—as you see them now—even further. This kind of iteration here and elsewhere in the planning process will help make your final plan as firm and accurate as current facts and forecasts will allow.

All three parts of your analysis should be in hand now: (1) the background, (2) the performance data (to include pricing), and (3) the potential for growth. One final step, before you begin drawing conclusions from your analysis, is to set forth the assumptions on which you're basing your analysis, conclusions, and—ultimately—objectives.

In the main, your assumptions should deal with things like: the availability of budget and staff called for in the plan; the factors in the economy (gas prices, employment levels, inflation rates) that could impact results significantly, social policy (you are a marketer for a number of homes for the disabled and assume that government-funding subsidies will remain unchanged), and the political climate (you assume that the current friendly local-government administration will not be replaced by unfriendly forces in the election to be held midway through execution of your annual plan). Make sure to point these out carefully to your superior in your joint review of the plan.

CONCLUSIONS/OBJECTIVES

The conclusions from your step-by-step analysis form the base for the very heart of your marketing plan—measurable objectives. By now you have a good idea what areas the objectives should cover, so it's best to formulate the conclusions in categories to match the objectives. It's not necessary or reasonable to have a perfect match right down the line, but there should be at least one conclusion from the analysis to support each objective.

Keep your goals in mind as well when you formulate the conclusions and corresponding objectives. The objectives, in fact, are the measurable means by which you eventually hope to achieve the goals. Awareness and use of the service, attitudes toward service, sale of a prime product (like a monthly pass), and numbers of inquiries in response to a special service or product are standard and meaningful objectives, particularly in the public sector, which needs a number of surrogates for the private sector's main measure—ROI.

Objectives should be attainable, clear, dated (a deadline), acceptable to peers and—most of all—measurable, or at least lay the base for subsequent measurement. For example, an objective that would work for virtually any public-sector agency is to raise public awareness of the service from 60 to 80 percent by year-end and to increase those who rate it good to excellent from 55 to 70 percent by year-end. This assumes a base measurement. If you're just starting primary research then the objectives are to establish base measurements of awareness and attitudes.

A common mistake is to set objectives that are beyond the scope of your group's responsibilities or ability to influence. This can occur, for instance, if you identify an innovation that will fall primarily to the planners to develop and implement, with promotional assistance from you. This possible pitfall is another reason why it's essential to be in close communication with your peers throughout the planning process.

It goes without saying that the objectives should be spread evenly among the customer service, promotion, and other functions that may reside in the marketing group. This is a strong tool for creating that desired balance in your marketing team.

In setting objectives, be realistic but reach a bit beyond what you believe you can attain in a given year (take into account the impact of innovation and promotion). If you're in the healthy position of negotiating annual objectives with your superior (rather than doing them in a vacuum), he or she is sure to ask for more rather than less. When that right level of challenge is achieved, the whole value and validity of objectives is advanced—to the benefit of all concerned. It takes time—and some trial and error—to find that "right" level, so don't be dismayed if the first try is too high or too low.

There's always the question: "How many objectives should I have?" The straight answer is no fewer than three or no more than six. Still it's impossible to generalize this guideline for all marketing groups because of their varied scopes. Two good rules are: (1) "do what you do well" and (2) "don't bite off more than you can chew," which is always a terrible temptation. Experience shows that the better agencies have fewer objectives. Remembering that marketing is not a quick-fix business, you must view the annual plan as a building block to three, four, or five years down the road. This is the point of overlap with the long-range plan, which is discussed in Chapter 6.

Having narrowed down to this focal point of direction for the coming year, you now begin broadening out again with the promotional strategies and projects that will dictate success, failure or a so-so performance.

6

promotion

DELIVER A

"KARATE CHOP"

Promotion must be the swift, hard-edged hand that gives your marketing effort a "karate chop" impact. As in karate, all force is marshalled through a demanding and disciplined mental process and brought to bear at a precise point.

Promotion, as defined in Chapter 1 and the Glossary, means paid-media advertising in concert with free-media support. Done correctly and in combination, promotion can rain powerful and telling blows in behalf of market penetration.

The initial step is developing solid attack strategies—rather than striking wildly in hopes of scoring some effective blows. Strategy development is the fun part of the planning phase. It's the place where you pose some conventional—and not-so-conventional—ways to carry out the objectives. This highly creative phase appeals to most marketers.

STRATEGIES/TACTICS

As the connecting links between the objectives and promotional projects, strategies are decisive factors in the ultimate success or failure of your marketing program. Generate a wide range of strategies and several alternatives in each area. This helps to surface the best strategies.

Specifically, if you're seeking to increase membership in an association, for instance, you must develop deliberate ways of achieving that objective. Some sample strategies, in an annual plan, might be to: (1) develop and present a slide show about the association to at least 500 prospective members by year-end; (2) conduct three seminars on subjects of interest to prospective members in the spring, fall, and winter; and (3) do a direct mailing to 100 selected prospects in the fall. All of these strategies are in support of the objective of increasing membership by a net figure of 200 by year-end. (Be conscious at this point about how well the strategies interrelate and how much you can do with anticipated staff and money.)

Strategic planning has a sweeping and grandiose ring to it. But in practice it comes down to devising the most effective ways to get your message to the desired market. More often than not, a strategy is as simple as a special brochure or slide show, when budget, staff resources, and other considerations are taken into account. Even so, make every effort to be innovative. Don't despair, though, if your strategies all seem pretty mundane because the real power in any set of strategies is how well you integrate and implement them.

The third tier of planning detail below objectives and strategies is tactics—the way in which you carry out the strategies. Tactics are best-described as a series of tasks. In the slide-show example, production of the show would be broken down into tasks keyed to the date you want to begin showing it. Once produced, you should have some monthly or weekly targets for the number of people who will have viewed it.

Draft your strategies and tactics using the same criteria as those for objectives: attainable, clear, dated, acceptable to peers, and measurable. The general guideline of a half-dozen objectives, at most, applies to strategies and tactics, too. Assuming six at each level, that expands to a grand total of 258! (6 + 36 + 216.) That's why fewer is better—if the whole process is not to fall under its own weight and complexity.

Once the objectives, strategies, and tactics are set, it's helpful to do a chronological summary, beginning with the earliest deadline. You can do separate objective, strategy, and tactics deadline summaries or lump everything into one long list. The important thing is to have a constant picture of what deadlines are at the top of the list and not rely on yourself or others to go looking through the plan every couple of days to see what's due. It won't happen. And that's how brush fires begin.

This is a super-critical juncture. Take a hard look at that long list of things you are about to promise to do. If it's more than you believe you can do with available time, dollars, and staff—"cut the cloth to fit." Combine, eliminate, delay a year—anything to avoid trying to do too much and turning your karate chop into a feeble slap. In limiting yourself, there's also more time to spend on perfecting the quality of the remaining work.

The true test of how many dollars you need is the amount—in your judgment—that it will take to meet the objectives. If you're already over some arbitrary limit and feel there are projects you need to do but can't afford, get your case together and go see your superior. Chances are good you'll get more money, especially if you have been building rapport. Settling on the right final list of projects, in light of objectives and strategies, is the lead marketer's biggest responsibility. Be aware that the package of projects that you go with are the product of all of your planning and your hope for a high-impact promotional program.

One of the best ways to get the most mileage from your time and money is to be aware of what others in the field are doing that worked. It also helps you avoid reinventing the wheel—a bureaucratic blunder every bit as bad as wasting good research information. An excellent example of building economically on another's success is the "Pass Plus" program shared by the Seattle and Portland transit systems. The program to get participating merchants to offer discounts on goods or services with the presentation of

Figure 8.   A sample Pass Plus card (Reproduced with permission of the Tri-Met Transit System).

a monthly bus pass began in Seattle with more than 150 participants.

Six months later, having borrowed virtually all of the sales materials and the name from Seattle's successful program, Portland introduced Pass Plus (Figure 8) in its service area with more than 300 participants. Think of the time and dollars that would have been wasted if Portland had chosen to invent its own wheel. What's more, they took a winner and made it even better, with relative ease.

RULES OF THUMB

Rules of thumb for your promotional budget as well as all marketing activities are indispensible in selling the budget to superiors. In the transit industry—of the total system operating budget—about .5 percent was reasonable for media advertising and sales promotion activities and about 4 percent was a fair figure for all marketing activities, including promotion. These heuristic guidelines, besides helping in your own planning, give added comfort to board members and chief executives. It's human nature to feel a little bit better about something (even if you oppose it) if "that's what other folks are doing."

Because of their interrelationship, it is wise to develop a general budget ratio for customer-service and promotional activities. In the transit industry a 2-to-1 ratio is reasonable, but it could vary widely in other areas of the public sector. The important thing is to establish a ratio and maintain it as a means of helping to preserve promotional dollars, in like proportion to customer-service dollars, in the event of a budget cutback. Any device you can use to demonstrate and defend the interdependence of these two key functions is useful, and budget is one of the best.

The leading example of a promotional project is a multimedia campaign with at least two waves in a year and two or more flights within each wave. A project can range from this most expensive effort to the slide show or a sales-promotion event, which are much less costly but also far less impactive. The promotional program should encompass all functions in your group. This is where the contribution of each unit of your marketing team is demonstrated.

THE SUMMARY SHEET

The promotional program summary chart (Figure 9), or "milestone chart," is unquestionably the single most important sheet in your entire annual marketing plan. Begin yours in rough form and perfect it from there. This chart will serve many vital and varied purposes:

• A snapshot of the array of projects you propose to implement (note that the campaign gets down to the level of the media mix)

Project	J	F	M	A	M	J	J	A	S	O	N	D	J	Budget ($ in thousands)
Campaign														
Paid television														125
Radio														50
Newspaper														25
Transit														15
Direct mail														10
(Subtotal)														(225)
Sales promotion														
Point of purchase														5
Booths														5
Door to door														5
(Subtotal)														(15)
Public relations														
Slide show														1
Graphics/style manual														1
Legislative kit														.5
(Subtotal)														(2.5)
Customer service														
Rate increase														1.5
Basic brochure														2
(Subtotal)														(3.5)
Other														
Contingency														4
Research/plan														20
Evaluation report														—
	* (Last year)												(This year) *	Totals 270

* Available effective date

Figure 9. This simple but effective form of summary chart gives a snapshot of all major projects and budgets in the marketing group over a program year.

85

- An estimate of the budget allotted to each project (a breakdown by periods of the year is optional)
- An overview of the timing of the projects individually, and in relation to each other
- A corresponding view of the low points in your promotional intensity, indicating where you should fill, if desirable and possible (most often the decision is to heavy-up the high points)
- A perspective on staff time demands and additional staff needs
- In final form, a ready reference for you, your staff, and your consultants (if any), and a succinct presentation piece for important audiences like your superior, board members, peers, and professional marketing groups.

A number of redrafts will be necessary to move from rough to final form. You'll find that this is an extremely easy and focused format that puts your whole promotional picture in bold relief. The ongoing value of this format— and the essence of it as well—is the overview that it provides of the intensity and continuity of your total program.

Promotional intensity and continuity are like an undulating ocean; the troughs give strength to the powerful waves that build and crest from them, only to return to the troughs. The waves—as they're, in fact, called in promotion—vary in strength themselves. This is because of the range of options available to you—from total media saturation of a market, to heavying-up in one medium, to selective buys that target only specific segments, and many more. But your program must move inexorably on—like the sea.

The cumulative effect of even high-impact campaigns takes time (as much as two years to build—from increasing levels of awareness, to the point where people decide to try your service and, finally, (hopefully) through deep market penetration). The lag-time is longest with committed non-users—if you get them at all. One program year must blend with the next. As with research, the main value of promotion is its effect over time. That's why there's no true quick-fix in the marketing business.

CONSULTANT RELATIONS

If you do plan to use consultants, this is the place to bring them aboard. You clearly need such a team if you plan a major multimedia campaign. The customary form is a full-service agency team, headed by an account executive assigned to you as the client.

One major caveat—if you've never worked with consultants. Give consultants *only* the responsibility to come back to you with a product for approval. Never delegate authority for implementation of a program to a consultant. That authority belongs to you and can't be delegated. You'll find that out very quickly if you do try to delegate your authority to a consultant and the program fails.

The consultant relationship can be painful or pleasant—beginning with the selection process. Here are some do's and don'ts aimed at ensuring fairness and objectivity in choosing a consultant:

* Do prepare specifications on the work to be done over what period of time and incorporate these into a request for proposals (RFP) with selection criteria and a schedule. Some agencies do not require bidding for small contracts, but specifications are helpful in any case. Bidding even for small jobs can help you get the best expertise available. On large contracts, some agencies begin with a re-

quest for qualifications (RFQ) as a first step before asking for actual proposals.

- Do set up a board of no fewer than three voting members to review the proposals, and interview finalists, if the work is bid.

- Do prepare grading sheets listing the selection criteria from the RFP so that all members are doing the evaluation from the same perspective.

- Do keep notes from the selection meeting and write a memo to file (or others who may need to be informed) stating the reasons for the selection of a particular consultant. There is always the possibility that a losing competitor will protest (if only to you over the telephone). It's good to have the reasons for the decision clearly in mind—even if you don't share them fully with the complaining party.

- Don't discuss anything about one consultant's presentation with one of the other competitors—even if both lost. In fact, "mum's the word" is an excellent motto in all matters concerning consultant selection.

- Don't accept any of the proposals if all are inferior or fall below your expectations. It's your neck on the block, remembering that you can't lay the ultimate responsibility (blame) on a consultant who doesn't perform.

- Do prepare and execute a performance contract carefully, with assistance from legal counsel.

- Do keep a list of the names and telephone numbers of consultants who have performed well for you in the past and those who express interest in future work.

The consultant contract for promotion is likely the largest you'll deal with, so you want the most for your money.

Since you're paying for highly specialized talent, it's best to bring the agency team in at a point where the promotional schedule is jelled—but not set. With that framework, the consultant can devote maximum time and attention to creating, producing, and delivering the many parts of the campaign. One reason you want the schedule in a jelled—rather than hard—state is that the consultant should have the ability to question and to have you modify strategies, projects, and—most certainly—elements of the media mix, if warranted. This, of course, comes after the consultant has studied the situation analysis and all relevant research in the plan thoroughly. If you did your planning well to this point, the consultant should be only too ready to begin putting together the campaign, or other projects for which he or she was hired.

Here the consultant becomes part of the team, just like your staff, and should be subject to the same production controls. It works best when there is a person on each side (yours/consultant's) as the day-to-day point of contact. Encourage the consultant to have at least one other person fully up to speed on the project, just as another in your office should be.

You can help the consultant do the best job by: (1) outlining clear project objectives (as you did with the researchers), (2) knowing the production process so you can evaluate the impact of change requests before you make them and know when to make such demands, and (3) paying them by the deadlines set in your contract (another place where the accountants can be of assistance if a check gets delayed).

As one respected colleague with long experience in advertising and promotion said: "Speed. Cost. Quality. Pick any two. You're kidding yourself if you try to get a consultant to deliver all three." Still, you must try.

For the best chance to get maximum results from your

relationship, the following expectations should be outlined to the consultant at the start:

- Brief meeting summaries, including major decisions—if any.
- The fewest possible attendees at meetings, but certainly all who have a direct role.
- Concise and orderly presentations. (If your consultants can't do that, their work product is sure to turn out the same.)
- At least two alternatives when it comes to campaign themes. If nothing else, this forces some discussion of the relative merits of the two and sharpens your idea of why you decided on the one you did. (Don't get too hung-up here. Repetition in multiple media and the media you choose to convey it are the crucial factors to a theme's success.)
- A distribution plan for nonbroadcast or print media. (Award-winning materials are worthless if they don't get into the hands of those they were intended for.)
- A detailed media plan, anytime the project involves the broadcast and print media.

Definitely look to a consultant for media buying. It's another of those science/art combinations and carries the greatest potential for literally multiplying the impact of a campaign. Given equal and adequate amounts of money, a good media planner/buyer can make a campaign, and a bad one can break it.

The science of media buying is in knowing the reach (how many people or homes are exposed to a given medium in a given period) and frequency (how often they're reached in that period) of the respective media. It's in knowing the characteristics of day-parts (see Glossary) and who's listening or watching during these various day-parts. And it's also in knowing the capabilities and limitations of each medium in relation to your service, and their arbitron ratings, circulation figures, availabilities, placement schedules, closing dates—and much more.

The art of media buying is in using these scientific tools to select the right media (means) to get the right message to the right markets at the right time—having come down to the very essence of the marketing action. The good buyers will have solid connections with "reps" from the various media in your service area and be able to take advantage of buying opportunities as the project is under way that were not available earlier.

In the computer age, the art is made somewhat easier by the speed with which the scientific data can be retrieved and massaged in infinitely greater depth and detail than during the manual era. You should have the media plan in plenty of time to review, discuss, and comprehend it before giving the go-ahead to launch a campaign. A key indicator of campaign strength is the number of gross rating points (GRPs) (see Glossary) it generates. These take on more significance when they're tracked from campaign to campaign because you can compare known quantities from your own experience. In this high-tech area of advertising, the GRPs are your best check on the sufficiency of the media plan.

ABOUT THEMES

Everyone, it seems, is a self-annointed genius in coining promotional themes (slogans). These creative contributions somehow seem to flow most freely at social gatherings. But

you can be accosted almost anywhere by someone who si-
dles up and says: "Hey, I have just the theme for you . . . ."

This comes, of course, from theme bombardment in the
broadcast media. In the public sector, the marines' "A Few
Good Men" was both a theme and a position statement and
"defined" its competitors in the other armed services as
well. "Metro (transit). It's Easy." was both a theme and
position. The army's "Be All that You Can Be" was simply a
theme. A comparison in the private sector: 7-Up's "The Un-
cola" was a theme/position that also defined the competition. Coke's "It's the Real Thing," by contrast, was simply a
theme. There's a subtle distinction between theme and position, but it should be clearer now how a theme can also be
a positioning statement and even define the competition. A
line incorporating all three elements will be the most effective.

Themes are important but for different reasons than
well-meaning laymen realize. Most people think cleverness
is the only criterion. They overlook the fact that a good
theme must stand up to frequent repetition without becoming trite or offensive and accurately represent the service or
product. It also should be extendable (flexible), if possible.
For example, a midwest transit system used the theme
"Take Me, I'm Yours," which extended to other uses like
"Take Me to the Opera," "Take Me to Work," and "Take Me
to School." Extendability isn't a must, but it helps the line
wear well.

The real value of a theme is using it to tie the various
elements of your campaign and overall marketing program together. Again, the effectiveness of a theme is not so
much its cleverness as it is the number of times it's repeated through the right media. Consider also how effectively it will work in each medium you plan to use in your
promotional program (e.g., some themes are too visual to be
effective on radio).

The best of all worlds is a clever, durable theme that also establishes a position, defines the competition, is extendable, and works well in all elements of your media mix. Whatever the theme, it—like the objectives, strategies, and projects—must be the product of a disciplined thought process, founded on research.

PRODUCTION POINTERS

As you proceed with the consultants on production, here are some other points to keep in mind:

- *Good Taste.* In all presentations of draft materials or "comps," be alert to nuances in the words or artwork that may irritate or even offend your many publics—particularly the board—who will be looking at the final product, to be sure, although they may not say anything to you. Good taste is a must in public-sector marketing.
- *Accuracy.* Make sure that what's written or pictured is accurate in relation to your service. Even "nit" mistakes can detract mightily from the credibility of your message.
- *Ethics.* Don't *ever* overpromise in your theme or supporting copy. If there's one thing worse than advertising a bad product, it's overpromising on it. Not only will those who are enticed to buy do it once—and never again— they'll get mad about being misled and try to get even by bad-mouthing your service to anyone who'll listen.
- *Plain Talk.* Most catchy names for things don't communicate well. While lots of people liked the name Magic Carpet for Metro Transit's free-bus-ride area, it took two paragraphs of copy to explain—before it was changed to simply the Ride Free area. People want to know—first—

how to use your service. Put the cuteness in the ad copy, not the names or titles of activities or services.

- *Quality.* Stress quality in all elements. It's true that quality only costs a little bit more. If you only have so much money to work with, and it comes down to doing that important brochure on coated stock in two colors or photocopying it on thin paper in black and white, find somewhere else to save a couple of dollars and go for the quality version.

- *Packaging.* This is an essential part of the marketer's art.

The public-sector marketer is packaging whether making a presentation to the board, directing production of a range of promotional materials, or overseeing the design of staff apparel or vehicle markings. Two practical aids here are having up-to-date and approved graphics and style manuals for the agency and having the graphics unit under marketing's control.

Your marketing plans are another packaging opportunity. From cover to cover, they should be crisp, concise, easily understood, and—thus—easily used. If you have mounds of data and tables, put them into an appendix for those who need the information. Use only essential and summary charts in the body of your plan so that it doesn't get bogged down in unnecessary detail.

FINISHING THE PLAN

For now, you still have some sections to complete for the annual plan. One is a section describing each of the projects briefly. Explain the objective, or objectives, it supports, what it involves, how it will be carried out, when, and by whom. Have those responsible for the projects do the write-ups. Put this section into the plan after the objectives section and before the program-summary sheet, so the summary will be more meaningful when the reader gets to it.

After the summary, provide a total marketing-group budget, showing the authorizations for each function. It's a good idea to show comparisons with two or three previous years' budgets as well. The more perspective you can give your plan throughout—in relation to previous experience—the more valuable it will be to you and others.

The last section of the annual plan sets forth how you will conduct your evaluation and your process for updating the plan (discussed in Chapter 8). For the long run (if you hope to have one) nothing is more important than the evaluation bridge into the next year's plan. At this point, you have three important things to think about. First, review and revise your annual plan one last time and get the buy-off from your peers and superior, in that order. Second, at the same time, you will be developing project plans and beginning work on the early projects, particularly the promotional campaign if you propose to do one. And third, you need to begin work on the long-range plan, if it wasn't done first. (See Appendix B.)

Much of the long-range plan groundwork was laid with your work on the situation analysis, plus any projects that didn't make it when you cut the cloth to fit for the annual plan and that you still want to do. The long-range plan is where the esoteric and evolving field of futurecasting is fully employed, along with the more traditional forecasting. Futurecasting deals with the softer business of crystal-balling megatrends and megaforces that will shape your situation—and indeed the world—in the years and decades ahead. Books like *Megatrends* and *The Third Wave* give those unfamiliar with the subject some good insights, but this is again the province of specialists. Some agencies have trained futurists on staff, as well as forecasters. Forecasting, as indicated in Chapter 5, relates more to hard-number projections in whatever units of measure you use. Your long-range plan should incorporate a studied analysis of future trends and projections beyond that provided in the annual plan. This, most likely, will require at least some outside advice.

You also are building on and blending with the annual plan in the area of goals and objectives, particularly the latter. You should have at least one objective in each of the goal areas for years two through five (if five is your "horizon" year). The horizon is extended a year, each year, after you complete your annual plan. With strategies to support the objectives, and any potential innovations, you have about all that's necessary. The purpose of the long-range plan is to keep your eye on the forest and not lost in the trees of this year and next.

The project plan, on the other hand, has just the opposite purpose. It gets into explicit detail on at least the big projects (and preferably even the smaller ones) listed in your promotional-program summary. With a half-dozen or more balls in the air at once in the promotional phase, you can't be too careful about ensuring that everyone knows his or her responsibilities and deadlines on each project. Appendix C provides a good working outline for a project plan. It can be as brief as one or two pages for a small project or run to a dozen or more for big ones. Keep in mind that the project plan, like the others, is a tool to help you produce better results, not an end in itself.

Do your plans carefully, communicate them, and then get on with implementation—the place where so many well-meaning marketers fall short.

7

implementation

CONDUCT THE CONCERT

Implementation is a function all its own, which too few marketers realize. As a result, the best-laid plans often go awry or fail to achieve their full potential from pure neglect. As the lead marketer, you should think like a musical conductor—orchestrating all of the activities involved in implementing the marketing plan.

The conductor must produce a symphony of sound through a blending of instrumental music; the marketer must deliver a desired result through a synergy of individual actions. This requires rapt attention to an array of responsibilities. Some are more obvious and easier to achieve, others are more subtle and take time to master.

Overall, today's marketing practitioner faces two extremes: (1) the academic approach steeped in systems analysis and mathematical models and (2) the gut-level, intuitive approach, which has been the more popular in all marketing—if the truth were known. The marketer who can combine the best of both into an approach that doesn't get too immersed in academe or succumb too quickly to the gut-feel will be contributing to progress in public-sector marketing. In plain terms, those who can blend the science and art of marketing will have the best chance of success.

THE SIMPLER THINGS

The simpler responsibilities are to continue to communicate, coordinate, and cooperate at all levels. If you did the preparatory steps right, then your job should be getting easier. Yet, as the conductor you must keep your eyes and ears attuned for the missed beat, the discordant sound, and the opportunity to amplify a high note.

You are using your management controls to the fullest at this point. Manage by exception as you direct the plan implementation. The theme concepts that weren't delivered when the schedule said they would be, the brochure that got through the blue-line stage without your signoff, the television spot that didn't play in the time slots called for in the media plan—all are red flags that require your attention and remedy. If not remedied when slightly out of sync, these small elements will combine to lessen the impact of your entire program.

Get out of your office during working hours and sense for yourself how the program is being received by the public. Talk to the employees at the distribution outlets; talk to the customers. Are people reacting to your message as you expected they would? Is it moving them to action? Are there problems? Are the materials getting into their hands as the distribution plan intended?

These questions and others will lead you to think about ways to intensify the promotional impact—even as the program's in progress. There are many possibilities—finding the money to go to full-color on that very important brochure, directing the media buyer to shift some dollars from print to a new television series where the impact will be many times as great, identifying several more distribution outlets in the heart of your market area. When subordinates come up with a good suggestion, make it their idea and give them the credit. Any new ideas must be incorporated into the process carefully, without disrupting the process or countermanding the efforts of those trying to follow through on original plans.

This is all the work of the marketing conductor. While it's seemingly simple, the importance of this kind of monitoring and minor fine-tuning is too often unappreciated. Besides losing opportunities for greater program impact, inattention during implementation can lead to the need for a major change of course.

A MAJOR CHANGE?

The going gets tougher if you reach a point where you must make a major change for the long-term good. That may mean a change in people, plans, or projects—any or all of the elements you're responsible for orchestrating. Temporary disruptions are disappointing, but if it takes a major action to avoid a pending problem, *do it* and recoup later, rather than fail badly now. This is especially true if you're just beginning a full-fledged marketing program.

Only you can be the judge of when you must act. A ripple of complaints about a campaign from board members, the public, or the media are early-warning signals that must be heeded. Don't jump to change if you feel you're on firm ground, but if any of the aforementioned groups (not to mention your boss) do begin to complain—and deep-down you agree with them—it's time to do something. Stop. Think it through. Consult with others. Then act.

If you do make a major change, do it decisively and thoroughly. Changes are not uncommon—particularly in an aggressive marketing program with an alert manager who's not sitting back letting the plan unfold as it may. The big secret of success—if not survival—is the quality of your follow-up. (It's more important how you followed-up than how you fouled-up!) As an example, if one of your three new 30-second radio or television spots offends a particular group or the public in general, pull it from the rotation, despite the sunk cost. Above all, don't let your ego get in the way of making the right decision in the public's behalf. A follow-up letter or even a meeting with the complainants is in order. If the "anti" reaction is general, a letter to the editor of the local newspapers explaining your point of view (perhaps apology) and/or corrective action is advisable.

Some changes are almost inevitable and a big reason

why you must remain fully aware during implementation. Often the conditions that create the need for quick adjustments to a project, or the entire program, are totally unforeseen. The gas crunch of the mid-1970s was a prime example. It hit with lightning speed, forcing marketers of every variety to shift gears rapidly. Just recognize that making a major change requires keeping faith with all the planning that went before. Save what you can, modify what you must.

THE SUBTLETIES

Anticipation, timing, and tone are three subtleties that a marketer must master to become truly proficient and effective.

Anticipation is born of constant awareness of all external and internal factors affecting the program. (No marketer can succeed without consuming large doses of daily news and information.) It's your responsibility, as the production and projects unfold, to spot the lagging elements and to get them back on schedule with a word here and a suggestion there. Done wrong, you can do more damage than good. Done right, you're merely doing your job and adding to the impact of the total program.

Timing is the key to achieving karate-chop impact. It's an absolute necessity where many elements must be brought to bear simultaneously to create synergy and, in turn, greater impact. Executing successive flights in a multimedia promotional campaign is a stern test of timing. Most important of all is having things happen when they were planned to happen and not accepting excuses for any delays that affect other program elements.

Tone is basic to true marketing artistry. It's difficult to define, but the accomplished marketer can spot, almost instinctively, the word or type face or sound that might convey a misimpression—or the same nuances that can enhance impact with only the slightest modification. Tone says a lot about a public agency. In pursuit of impact, don't become too strident or outspoken in your promotional message. You want the public to perceive you as a high-quality agency in the first instance, as well as for the long haul. Listen carefully for that inappropriate tone in the content of any messages you're preparing. Like an individual, an agency should develop a personality and voice that are consistent, reliable, and cordial.

While striving for ever-higher levels of achievement as a conductor, remember that in the real world of public-sector marketing you're often operating without the kind of score that guides your musical counterpart and without the audience to appreciate your artistry. When mediocrity will suffice, who really cares about striving for perfection? Perhaps only you do. But that should be enough.

DO IT YOUR WAY

Since this is a marketing—not a management—guide, the way you actually perform as the conductor is left to your own personal approach. This book is more concerned with what you should be doing rather than how you should be doing it. Hopefully, your style and aspirations will mesh with those of the agency, and particularly the leadership. Realize that there is inherent risk in any bureaucratic position where you must be forceful—and a catalyst for change—in order to do your job well. Don't shrink from the responsibility for that reason. And extend the freedom to take risks (the right to fail) to your staff and consultants as well if you value making something unique happen.

As implementation is the orchestration of all the planning and production efforts, evaluation is the view of how it "played" with your publics. All endeavors need outside and objective opinions to validate their effectiveness. This is especially true of something as subjective and sensitive as public-sector marketing.

Without evaluation there can be no certainty that this year's program was a success and no basis on which to build next year's program with increased confidence.

8

---

evaluation

REPORT THE RESULTS

Evaluation is the phase that follows the planning and promotional phases of the marketing cycle and links the three
into a continuous process.

Early-on, evaluation is informal—even intuitive—as
you begin assessing the effectiveness of individual projects
almost from the first days of implementation. The feedback
to staff and superiors is largely verbal, although you may
be tracking and recording some numbers in response to new
products, like a monthly pass or home-energy-check offer.

More formality comes with a sequence of brief reports
(monthly is good) that begin circulating the results that
you have in hand. These come from the numbers you've
been gathering in the informal stage, feedback through
outside sources and the media, and information gleaned
from calls to the customer-service staff. Anything that
helps get a handle on how the projects are doing is suitable.
Be sure these reports get into the hands of those who had a
lead role in preparing the plans and those who have a lead
role in implementing various projects.

LOOK TO OBJECTIVES

The highest level of formality is beginning to track progress against the objectives that are the heart of your annual marketing plan. In the evaluation section of your annual plan you should spell out the techniques you will use
in measuring results on each objective. This obviously will
involve use of your baseline research study results in areas
like awareness and attitudes toward your service. This may
need to be supplemented by other posttesting techniques,
especially if you are just beginning the marketing process
and don't have complete baseline research as a follow-up to
a promotional phase.

You should present the results of your objectives to your superior and the board after the program year is completed. If you did a good job of making the objectives measurable, then evaluation should be relatively easy. Without measurable objectives—or any objectives at all—your evaluation of the marketing program is highly subjective and debatable because there are no acknowledged standards of success or failure. And you deserve the flack you'll get. Moreover, it encourages what one colleague calls "retroactive criteria"—those imposed after the fact by the chief executive and/or board when there are none at the beginning.

Evaluation based on objectives that all parties agreed on at the outset focuses discussion on those objectives. If you have positive results to report, agency leaders can see the return on their investment and it's bound to build confidence in the marketing program. Even if some or all of the numbers are negative you have a much clearer handle on the challenge than you do with no objectives and measures. Most superiors appreciate professionalism and realize it takes time to develop an effective marketing program.

Many marketers plan and promote well, yet fail in evaluation—and the cyclical process falls apart or gets badly out of sync as debate over the previous program drags on. Then you *are* in trouble. There are a few probable causes why some drop the ball on evaluation:

1. They become so consumed with the planning and promotional effort that they simply overlook evaluation as a distinct phase. (Make it a section in the annual plan.)

2. They don't particularly like the results and opt to keep quiet rather than report them. This is not a winning strategy. (No news is bad news.)

3. They fail to attach the kind of importance to the re-
    porting of results that it deserves—or that superiors
    attach to it. (For best results—report the results!)

THE COST-BENEFIT QUESTION

Because the public is in an ownership role, intangibles like
attitudes toward the service and awareness of it are legiti-
mate indicators of the benefits of your marketing program.
But if you don't identify them as objectives and can't measure them, then the sole standard of success is imposed by
superiors and the budget-makers. One of those retroactive
criteria is sure to be the old cost-benefit ratio—a comparison of the dollars you spent on promotion to get X number
of people to use the agency's service (or not use the service—as in the case of conservation-minded energy agencies or police and fire departments bent on reducing crime
and fires).

And there's the age-old debate in the public sector (and
much of the private as well) as to how many people would
have used the service anyway—without your marketing
efforts. This is a moot point—if you have capacity to offer,
products to sell, and an aggressive image to convey. If you
don't have the capacity, by all means pull back to basic
services—just as you would with a poor product.

I considered .5 percent of the total annual transit operating budget a reasonable amount to spend each year to tell
people about a service that cost nearly $100 million to run
and much more than that to build and buy. Perhaps your
figures and percentages aren't as dramatic and favorable,
but it's a good bet that they will be close—or that your
modest marketing budget may even sound smaller in com-

parison with your organization's total operating budget each year.

A pro-marketing board member once used this analogy during public questioning on the "return" from the Metro Transit marketing program. He said the discussion reminded him of the folly of building a beautiful new church and then failing to spend a little more for a bell so people from all around would know the church was there. An equally apt analogy is building a grocery store and continuing to add inventory rather than spend a reasonable amount on advertising to tell the people the store is there and what it has to sell.

If you don't use either the store or church analogies, *do* discipline yourself to report religiously! Although the circumstances may vary widely, reporting is the vehicle for keeping your marketing program intact and moving forward without interruption.

THE PROCESS SCHEDULE

Scheduling is fundamental to the rhythm of the overall program. It's impossible to deliver good results without close and continuing attention to the three main phases: planning, promotion, and evaluation. Figure 10 shows how all of the phases fit and flow in the cyclical process. Your phasing and process schedule will depend on the nature of your service. The key is to establish a schedule and keep it in sync.

It seems to work best to get your promotional phase on a calendar-year schedule as an anchor point. Next, plug in the all-important and time-consuming situation analysis. Then spot the reporting date at a time when the preceding

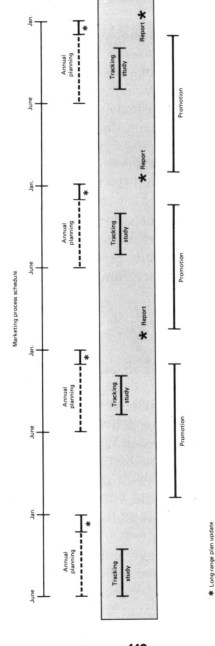

Marketing process schedule

Figure 10. This diagram depicts the planning, promotion, and evaluation (report) phases of the cyclical marketing process, with research (tracking) studies as the central part of the process.

* Long-range plan update

promotion program has been implemented and before the new one begins.

As mentioned earlier, it may be awkward but necessary to conduct your first baseline (tracking) research study even as you're preparing your first situation analysis—if you have neither. The second annual tracking study should fit neatly into the process the following year. (See Figure 10.)

The biggest stumbling block to good evaluation reporting is trying to provide too many facts. A factually overwhelming presentation is counterproductive. Think simplicity. It's hard work to distill many disparate facts into a succinct and logical story. Some people think that dazzling an audience with data is impressive. In fact, it shows that you were too lazy to boil it down into something meaningful and understandable.

REPORTING FORMATS

Chief executives and board members are busy people used to making decisions on the basis of brief but complete reports. A chairman of Boeing, the world's largest aerospace manufacturer, was noted for wanting issues needing his decision presented in a single page (and all of the facts had better be accurate!). One can only surmise the mounds of data that supported those single-page reports and how hard his staff must have worked to boil it down to a single page.

Besides the one- or two-page memo, there are a number of other standard reporting formats from which to choose in presenting the results of your program, or progress along the way. And most often it's a combination of these:

- A multipage report, with selected bar and pie charts and graphs and an executive summary, much like the suggested marketing plan format. This can be for a specific audience but most often is for wider distribution than any of the other formats discussed.

- Viewfoils, used on an overhead projector, are quick and economical to produce and work best with groups of 10 to 30. They lend an air of informality and afford more flexibility than either slides or videotapes.

- Flip charts, with an easel, also are fast and inexpensive to produce and have the same informality and flexibility as viewfoils. Of the two, viewfoils tend to focus attention on the subject matter more effectively because the room—or at least the part near the screen—is darkened.

- Slides, shown on a 35mm carousel projector, are best with groups larger than 30 and where you intend the presentation to be more formal (i.e., questions at the end of the presentation, rather than interspersed; high-level attendees).

- Videotape is becoming more popular as production costs get lower and the hardware for showing it less expensive and more portable. This medium is also a good way to inform employees in widely dispersed work sites about the upcoming promotional campaign, or other big projects.

With any of these formats the important thing is the content of your reports—its relevance to the objectives you set out to achieve, its accuracy, and its relationship to proposed future actions. Always keep that third point in mind because the major reason for reporting is to build a bridge to the next planning phase.

In all you present, make certain that you have reviewed and are knowledgeable about the material, especially if it was prepared by others. Nothing is more destructive of a good presentation than your inability to answer questions. The commonsense alternatives of saying, "I don't know, but I'll get you the answer," or calling on a subordinate for assistance are acceptable. However, nothing beats having the answers cold—and keeping them brief and simple, too. (Particularly watch bureaucratic jargon, and speak loudly for the benefit of the hard of hearing in the audience.)

Think packaging in any presentation. The best of information poorly packaged detracts badly from the overall effectiveness of a presentation or written report. Good graphics support is essential. And computers are a boon—with their ever-improving graphics capability to go along with exponential increases in the ability to massage data. If you're going to use computers, the evaluation phase is the place.

Response to presentations and reports will vary. The important thing is to speak in plain language and then to listen carefully and incorporate useful portions of what you hear into the next plan or project. There's no quicker way to win over an adversary than to have that person see at least some part of his or her idea or suggestion reflected in a future project. It helps even more if you remember to give credit—when credit is due. Moreover, in listening you'll get some sound suggestions from some surprising sources.

Undertake each such experience expecting to find allies rather than adversaries. If you meet with opposition, understand that accommodation of each others' views takes time and patience. As an advocate for an aggressive marketing program, the onus is on you to explain why you want to do certain things and to gain the support of the decision-makers who sit in judgment.

Above all, persevere in your reporting. Don't be disillusioned if your major presentation gets a poor reception. Follow-up. Go one on one, if necessary, with those who truly

don't understand or even openly oppose your program—or
some part of it. They still may not agree, but they will
appreciate the attention you showed—whatever their position outside or inside the organization.

The aim always in evaluation reporting is to provide a
smooth transition into the next promotional year. Without
permission to move ahead, you're stymied; with it, you're
flying high.

Assuming the latter, the marketing process has come full
cycle—only to continue.

9

the payoff

A GRATIFYING

CONTRIBUTION

The five rights of marketing can easily make a wrong, in the hands of an imposter or a careless practitioner. The pitfalls of getting the right service to the right markets at the right price by the right means at the right time are many and constant—even for an experienced marketer.

It's never easy because marketers are "point" people in forever unfamiliar territory. They operate in large measure on intuition. But they need some solid guidelines to deal instinctively and consistently with daily challenges, to maintain the offensive, and to forge an understanding and appreciation of their validity and value.

The five rights is such a set of guidelines, and there are others, which provided the central theme for each chapter in this book.

In each case, imagery was employed to help get the guidelines across and have them stick in your mind. Hopefully, the simile and metaphor will make it easier for you to remember that:

- *Structure Is a Crucial Consideration.* Like a football coach, pick the right people for the right positions before you begin playing.
- *Customer Service Takes Precedence Over Everything.* Built solidly, it's the launching pad for your marketing moonshot.
- *Without Research, You Aren't Doing Marketing.* Research is as inherent to marketing as your five senses are to you.
- *Planning Is Phase One of the Marketing Process.* It prevents brush fires and prepares you to deliver the marketing karate chop.
- *Implementation Is the Culmination of Planning and Pro-*

duction. Think of yourself as the conductor orchestrating the high-impact promotional program (phase-two).

- *Evaluation Is Phase Three.* The connecting link in the cyclical process of public-sector marketing.

The accompanying checklist, plan outlines, and Glossary are important aids to a disciplined approach and semantic understanding—the cornerstones to progress in public-sector marketing.

THREE PRINCIPLES

The day of marketing's recognition as a profession is somewhere down the road. But much progress can be made if all practitioners will apply the guidelines discussed and the three general principles of simplicity, quality, and perseverance in their daily work. While these are broad terms, there is an essence to each.

Simplicity boils down to organizing people and communicating plans in such a way that all of the team members can indeed perform as one when the action starts. Synergy begins with each individual clearly understanding (and accepting) his or her role. Figures 5 and 9 are especially helpful in achieving communication clearly and simply.

Quality is harder to define. It's consistency in packaging, coupled with high-caliber customer service; it's responsiveness and innovation; it's timing and tone. It's something you can identify more readily when you don't have it than when you do.

Perseverance should pervade all of your efforts. It is most needed in achieving and enhancing the marketing orientation of your organization. No challenge in public-sector marketing exceeds this one.

THE MARKETER'S IMAGE

The factors vital to your own personal success and happiness as a public-sector marketer are job knowledge, interpersonal relations, and cooperation. These are cornerstones of the image you convey to your associates in the agency.

   With the rising attractiveness of public-sector marketing as a career field, there's a corresponding need to become more and more proficient in the myriad scientific and artistic aspects of the business. This requires keeping current by reading on your own as well as on the job, joining professional organizations like the American Marketing Association, and seeking opportunities for special seminars or for-credit course work at local colleges or universities. In many cases, the agency will pay for at least part of the cost of this kind of advanced schooling. Besides being a necessity, professional growth builds respect.

The increased use of quantitative methods, mathematical modeling, and systems analysis require marketers to be comfortable and competent with numbers. This does not mean that you must be capable of doing that kind of work, only that you be able to understand, critique, and apply the results properly in the planning process.

The first stumbling block to success in any organization is poor interpersonal relations. If you're not ready to be reasonable, flexible, and accessible—get out of the public-sector marketing business, or don't get in. Use face-to-face contact as the preferred type of contact. The telephone's next. And memos are a last resort, for real communication, but they are useful to give direction or record important actions or discussions. Take the initiative in interpersonal communications whenever possible and it will pay big dividends.

The foremost of those dividends is cooperation. It's difficult for anyone at any level to withhold cooperation if you have taken the initiative repeatedly to communicate and cooperate with them. Cooperation means give-and-take quite often, particularly in a large organization where the number of interests are multiplied. But that doesn't mean giving in when you believe strongly that you're right. If mutual respect and communication are there, the impasses will be few and far between.

The practitioner-to-be can expect misconceptions from prospective employers. Be prepared for them to ask during an interview what brilliant marketing ideas you have for the "good ol' XYZ agency." Come now. Do they ask instant opinions of doctors, lawyers, or engineers? No. Never. They respect the fact that these professionals come with credentials and competence and would never render even a preliminary opinion without an opportunity to study the situation.

So it must be with marketers in the quest for progress toward professionalism. Ask about the organizational structure. Talk about the planning process. Tell the interviewer that the ideas will flow from the process. You can *guarantee* that. And you can be confident of delivering results if your new boss supports the approach. If he or she doesn't—think longer about taking the job, if it's offered.

THE OPPORTUNITY

It's safe to predict that for the foreseeable future, the public dollars will go where the marketing is good. The information era has brought ever-increasing competition among agencies for attention and support from the public that holds the purse strings. Services that are misunderstood or underused can count on coming up short in public-funding elections or at budget time in this new environment (assuming they deserve support and have unused capacity to begin with). If anything, competition will get more intense. The agencies that are aggressively seeking new customers and keeping the old ones satisfied will enjoy the public support. Those that ignore the new consumerism and fail to use the power of marketing in the public sector will be hard-pressed to succeed.

Among the enlightened leaders in bringing about the belated marriage of marketing and the public sector are the military (which outspends many major corporations in media advertising), transit systems, public health-care facilities, energy utilities, and public attractions, such as zoos, stadiums, and aquariums. Competition—if not survival—was or is at the root of much of this new marketing interest. The shift to a volunteer army made marketing imperative for the military. Energy agencies facing serious shortages had to teach old consumers new conservation tricks. The expenditures can range into the millions of dollars annually for campaigns using multiple media, including paid-television advertising. Bolstered by these front-runners, public-sector marketing is resolving its identity crisis and rising in recognition.

Through changing conditions a momentum is building. With better prepared practitioners, improved planning, and consistent performance—public-sector marketing can emerge even more quickly and easily and with greater benefit to more people.

For all involved or interested in public-sector marketing as a career, it's time to face facts. Public-sector marketing doesn't deserve its muddled and mediocre image. Unfortunately, as Pogo said: "We have met the enemy—and he is us." Even though this book seeks to remedy that, the turnaround will take time and tenacity.

A HIGH CALLING

In practice, the expert public-sector marketer has a high calling and can make a gratifying contribution. He or she embodies the talent and training to take the lead in:

* Preserving public services under siege, whether because of dwindling markets or high-handed treatment of the public
* Maintaining support for vital community services, such as transportation, energy, education, public safety, sanitation, health care, culture, and recreation
* Enhancing the image and effectiveness of services operating below their potential
* Winning public elections in behalf of worthy causes and candidates

I know from my own experiences, and those of my colleagues, that the results from the successful practice of public-sector marketing can be deeply gratifying: seeing people use your rejuvenated bus system more often and easily, knowing that millions of dollars in funding for essential services were made possible by your part in winning crucial public elections, watching sick people get needed medical care from a facility you helped to save from closure, hearing students talk excitedly about attending a college you helped bring back from the brink of bankruptcy, and seeing a community turn from conspicuous consumption of energy to conservation in response to your campaign. All these and more are the reasons that public-sector marketing is finally gaining attention and emerging as a career field. It's wide open and waiting for the right people (and the salary scales are improving as well).

THE FINAL ANALYSIS

In the final analysis, public-sector marketing has fallen far short of its own potential because it has not yet come to know itself. How then could outsiders understand? The role of the public-sector marketer is to orchestrate an array of people and plans into amplified action on behalf of present or potential customers and the tax-paying public at large. The very complexity of the challenge demands a disciplined process and dedicated leadership.

This book provides the definition and practical process to bring about rapid progress in your organization and in the beckoning field of public-sector marketing. It's in your hands—or at least within your grasp.

appendix a

MARKETING
AUDIT CHECKLIST

This checklist of 100 questions, from information in Chapters 1–9, will help marketing practitioners evaluate the situation in any public-sector organization. The ratings call for highly subjective judgments, based on experience and personal perspective. The questions are intended to illuminate the most important points and to isolate the areas that need the most and earliest attention.

The composite checklist represents an audit report on an existing program or one about to be launched. A score of less than 200 for an existing program indicates a big challenge ahead. Analyze and prioritize the lowest scores and begin the improvement efforts there.

CHAPTER 1
Public-Sector Marketing

	Low (No) 1	Moderate (No opinion) 2	High (Yes) 3
Is there clear understanding that you are a public agency?	____	____	____
Is there a clear understanding of what marketing is in your agency?	____	____	____
Does marketing have a hand in shaping the service?	____	____	____
Does marketing have superiors' support?	____	____	____

	Low (No) 1	Moderate (No opinion) 2	High (Yes) 3

How would you rate your agency's competence in these marketing functions (even though they are assigned elsewhere in the agency)?

	Low	Moderate	High
Customer service	___	___	___
Research	___	___	___
Advertising	___	___	___
Sales promotion	___	___	___
Public relations	___	___	___
Media relations	___	___	___
Community relations	___	___	___
Government relations	___	___	___
Public affairs	___	___	___
Graphics	___	___	___
Distribution	___	___	___
Internal readiness:			
Staff knowledge	___	___	___
Staff training	___	___	___
Appearance of staff	___	___	___
Appearance of facilities	___	___	___

Subtotal ___

CHAPTER 2
Organization

	Low (No) 1	Moderate (No opinion) 2	High (Yes) 3
Rank your structure from pyramidal (high) to scattered (low).	____	____	____
Are the power and regard for each group balanced?	____	____	____
Can you talk to your superior about structure?	____	____	____
What is the quality of your relationship with the planning group?	____	____	____
How satisfactory is the structure of your marketing group?	____	____	____
How adequate is the staffing of your marketing group?	____	____	____
How would you rate the quality of your job descriptions?	____	____	____
How adequate are these management controls?			
Budget tracking	____	____	____
Deadline tracking	____	____	____
Performance tracking	____	____	____

	Low (No) 1	Moderate (No opinion) 2	High (Yes) 3
How adequate is your computer-support system?	____	____	____
How would you rate your spending authority?	____	____	____
How informed are you about the mission and goals of your agency?	____	____	____
Subtotal			____

CHAPTER 3
Customer Service

	Low (No) 1	Moderate (No opinion) 2	High (Yes) 3
How aggressive is your approach to customer service?	___	___	___
How would you evaluate your key customer services?			
Telephone information	___	___	___
Complaint handling	___	___	___
Walk-in center(s)	___	___	___
Basic printed material	___	___	___
How would you evaluate your special services?	___	___	___
How effective are your customer-service management controls?	___	___	___
How would you rate your agency's marketing orientation?	___	___	___
Top management	___	___	___
Other (nonmarketing) groups	___	___	___
Individual staff members	___	___	___

Subtotal ___

CHAPTER 4
Research

	Low (No) 1	Moderate (No opinion) 2	High (Yes) 3
How good is your secondary research?	____	____	____
Have you used primary research in support of market planning?	____	____	____
How would you rate the quality of the study reports you have received?	____	____	____
How good is your information in the major research categories?	____	____	____
Awareness/attitudes	____	____	____
Market segments/behavior/demand	____	____	____
Most effective messages/media	____	____	____
How would you rate your effectiveness in using research results?	____	____	____
How would you rate the quality of your baseline (tracking) data?	____	____	____

Subtotal ____

CHAPTER 5
Planning

	Low (No) 1	Moderate (No opinion) 2	High (Yes) 3
Are you plagued with brush fires?	___	___	___
How would you rate your own planning mentality?	___	___	___
How would you evaluate the quality of your mission statement?	___	___	___
How would you evaluate the quality of your goals?	___	___	___
How would you evaluate the quality of your situation analysis?	___	___	___
How would you evaluate the market segmentation section of your situation analysis?	___	___	___
Does marketing have a hand in pricing the service?	___	___	___
How is the quality of your forecasting?	___	___	___
How do you rate on innovation?	___	___	___
How strong is your position statement?	___	___	___
How would you rate the quality of your objectives?	___	___	___

Subtotal ___

CHAPTER 6
Promotion

	Low (No) 1	Moderate (No opinion) 2	High (Yes) 3
How would you evaluate the quality of your strategies?	___	___	___
How would you evaluate the quality of your tactics?	___	___	___
Do you have rules of thumb for promotional spending?	___	___	___
How effectively have you summarized your promotional program on a single sheet?	___	___	___
How good a working relationship do you have with consultants?	___	___	___
How effective do you feel your positions/themes have been?	___	___	___
How would you rate your packaging?	___	___	___
How would you rate your plans?			
Annual	___	___	___
Long range	___	___	___
Project	___	___	___
Subtotal			___

CHAPTER 7
Implementation

	Low (No) 1	Moderate (No opinion) 2	High (Yes) 3
How well do you (lead marketer) fit the conductor model?	___	___	___
How well do your marketing-management controls work?	___	___	___
How effective are you at making needed minor program adjustments?	___	___	___
How decisively do you act when a major change is called for?	___	___	___
How well are the subtleties of your marketing program handled (anticipation/timing/tone)?	___	___	___
Are you prepared to face the risks that a marketer will encounter in being a catalyst for change?	___	___	___
		Subtotal	___

CHAPTER 8
Evaluation

	Low (No) 1	Moderate (No opinion) 2	High (Yes) 3
Do you have agreed-on objectives to use as the basis of your evaluation?	____	____	____
How well have you answered the cost-benefit question?	____	____	____
How well are your planning, promotional, and evaluation phases in sync?	____	____	____
How would you evaluate the key aspects of your reporting?			
Succinctness	____	____	____
Appropriateness of formats	____	____	____
Relevance to objectives	____	____	____
Accuracy	____	____	____
Bridge to future actions	____	____	____
How would you evaluate the over-all effectiveness of your reporting (knowledge, packaging, follow-up)?	____	____	____

Subtotal ____

CHAPTER 9
The Payoff

	Low (No) 1	Moderate (No opinion) 2	High (Yes) 3
How do you rate on delivering the five "rights?"			
Service	____	____	____
Markets	____	____	____
Price	____	____	____
Means	____	____	____
Timing	____	____	____
To what degree do you practice the principles of:			
Simplicity	____	____	____
Quality	____	____	____
Perseverance	____	____	____
How would you rate yourself on these qualities?			
Marketing knowledge	____	____	____
Interpersonal relations	____	____	____
Cooperation with others	____	____	____
How optimistic are you about the future of public-sector marketing?	____	____	____
How highly do you value public service?	____	____	____

	Low (No) 1	Moderate (No opinion) 2	High (Yes) 3

How interested are you in
public-sector marketing as a
career?   ____   ____   ____

                               Subtotal   ____

CHECKLIST TOTALS
Chapter 1 _____
Chapter 2 _____
Chapter 3 _____
Chapter 4 _____
Chapter 5 _____
Chapter 6 _____
Chapter 7 _____
Chapter 8 _____
Chapter 9 _____
Total _____

appendix b

ANNUAL AND LONG-RANGE
MARKETING PLAN OUTLINES

ANNUAL MARKETING PLAN OUTLINE

Table of contents	All elements in the plan and number of page where each is introduced
Introduction	Purpose and uses of the plan
Executive summary	Digest of important information in the plan
Mission/goals	Statement of agency purpose and direction
Situation analysis	Information on which the plan is based
Background	
Service description	Profile of service (product) provided
Market description	Population, households, income, occupation, and related data for service area
Major markets	Description of major markets for service (current and potential)
Major factors	Factors affecting the agency's delivery of service, including such elements as the economy, political/governmental, educational, social, and technological
Competitive environment	Direct or indirect competitors with the service offered

Organizational resources	Summary of staff and budget resources
Agency	Structure, staff capabilities, financial outlook, and funding sources
Marketing group	Structure, staff capabilities, and anticipated budget
Performance	
Use of service	Data on use of service (up to five years); characteristics of users, frequency of use, and related information
Primary research	Summary of findings from application of primary research techniques; includes awareness and attitudes/market-segment profiles, behavior and demand/messages, and media/and other areas of inquiry
Pricing	Current pricing structure, and alternatives (if appropriate)
Potential	
Forecast	Projections of service use for the plan year
Innovation	Proposed service/product innovations during the plan year

Positioning	Statement of the current marketing position (theme) and supporting reasons
Assumptions	Key factors from the analysis of the operating environment and organizational resources that are assumed in the plan
Conclusions	Statements of conclusions from the situation analysis
Objectives/strategies	Results to be produced and the strategies for achieving them
Promotional program	Program (individual projects) proposed to promote use/support of service
Project descriptions	Brief descriptions of individual projects
Program	Single-sheet matrix summarizing projects, budget and staffing needs, and schedule
Marketing group budget	Total budget by functional unit
Evaluation	Description of the methods that will be used in evaluation, the reporting process, and plan-update schedule

LONG-RANGE PLAN OUTLINE

Table of contents	Same as for annual plan
Introduction	Same as for annual plan (append and refer to current annual plan)
Executive summary	Same as for annual plan
Futurecast	Broad view of economic, political/governmental, social, technological, and other forces and trends that may affect your service in the future
Forecast	Projections of use through horizon year of long-range plan
Objectives	Objectives for each year from years two through the horizon year of your long-range plan set in the context of your goals
Strategies	Two or three strategies for each objective each year; these will be refined in the annual plan for that year
Other factors	Any other factors not covered in this or in the appended annual plan

appendix c

PROJECT

PLAN OUTLINE

PROJECT PLAN OUTLINE

Description	A concise summary of the project outlining the objective(s) it supports, what it involves, and how it will be carried out
Research	Relevant research information from the annual plan situation analysis and other sources
Position	A positioning statement using either the overall program position or a related position statement developed specifically for this project
Promotion	A listing, with brief descriptions, of the advertising, sales promotion, public relations, and other relevant activities that will be implemented in behalf of the project
Schedule/budget matrix	A single-page matrix similar to the program summary chart that shows the schedule of all project activities, budget for each element, and a total budget

Chronological deadline/
responsibility summary

A summary of task dead-
lines in chronological order with an indication of
the person responsible
for each task

Glossary

The following are definitions of terms used in the text of this book and others the practitioner will encounter frequently, with examples where appropriate. The definitions are practical interpretations of the terms, as one might hear them used in day-to-day public-sector marketing activities.

ACCOUNTABILITY: Clear designation of the individual responsible for the results of a project or program.

ACCOUNT EXECUTIVE: Advertising agency person responsible for all contacts with the client.

ADMINISTRATOR: High-level member of the bureaucracy charged with administering policy set by the board; also has policy-setting authority, as delegated by the board or an administrative superior.

ADP: Automated data processing; used on complex projects like budget preparation/media planning.

ADVERTISING: Paid message provided by a sponsor through various advertising media.

ADVERTISING MEDIA: The means by which an advertising message is delivered. The principal media include television, radio, newspapers, magazines, direct mail, billboards, transit, specialty items, brochures, flyers, and point-of-purchase displays.

AGENCY: Used here to describe either a public-sector organization or an advertising agency.

AGGRESSIVE: Active and strong pursuit of marketing objectives (contrasted with passive approach that keeps programs on the defensive).

AGREEMENT: Synonym for contract.

AMA: American Marketing Association (see *Associations*).

ANALYSIS: Systematic and rigorous review and interpretation of applicable information on a specific subject.

ANNUAL MARKETING PLAN: The marketer's primary—and most valuable—working tool, which sets forth the 12-month program of marketing activities (see *Appendix B*).

APPEAL: Sales message.

ARBITRON RATING: Automated rating of television program audience size via diaries and/or electronic devices placed in the home and connected with a central tabulating machine; product of American Research Bureau.

ART: Creative skill, both innate and acquired, as it relates to the practice of marketing—particularly program implementation (see *Science*).

ASSOCIATIONS: Professional organizations, like the AMA, whose purpose is to further the field of marketing; also a significant segment of the public sector (i.e., chambers of commerce and trade associations).

ATTITUDE: The public's beliefs and opinions about a particular service or product, or some aspect of it.

AUDIO-VISUAL: Sound and picture presentation devices, such as 35mm-slide and voice-tape units.

AUDIT: Systematic evaluation of a marketing program (see *Appendix A*).

AUTHORITY: The power to act or direct the actions of others by virtue of one's position in an organization; unlike responsibility, can (and should) be delegated.

AUTOMATIC DATA PROCESSING: See *ADP*.

AUTOMATIC SELLING: Direct sales of products through machines operated by the customer using currency, charge card, or other device.

AVAILS: Availability of time or space sold by an advertising medium.

AWARENESS: The public's knowledge or lack of knowledge about a service, or some aspect of it.

BANNER TABLES: Cross-tabulation statistical tables organized to compare a few key questions with many others.

BASELINE QUESTIONS: Questions asked in an initial study, then repeated in successive tracking studies in order to determine trends in public attitudes and awareness.

BENEFIT: A perceived value received from a service or product.

BIAS: In research, anything that interferes with the receipt of accurate information from a respondent; most often results from the inappropriate wording or communication of a question or bad sampling.

BID: A potential supplier's response to an advertised bid-call or a request for proposals.

BILLBOARD: Stationary outdoor advertising sign placed along major roadways, often illuminated from above or below; also, a typewritten television message (see *Videotext*).

BLUE-LINE: A final proof of printed material ready for production; so-called because of its one color—blue.

BOARD: The group responsible for making policy in the organization; often called councils or commissions in the public sector.

BOSS: See *Chief executive*.

BROADCAST MEDIA: A category of advertising media including television and radio.

BROCHURE: A pocket-sized printed piece (of varying sizes)

distributed personally, by mail, or in point-of-purchase displays.

BUDGET: The plan for expenditure of money for a particular project or program and staff over a specified period of time.

BULLETIN BOARD: A popular device in public agencies for display of internal information and appropriate external materials.

BUREAUCRACY: Administration of government through departments and divisions following a prescribed organizational structure and policies.

CAMERA-READY: Artwork and/or type paste-ups that need no further processing prior to final production.

CAMPAIGN: A multi media promotional effort conducted over a specified period of time, involving one or more waves (e.g., spring and fall waves of an annual promotional campaign) (see *Wave, Flight, Hit*).

CAR CARD: A large card containing an advertising message and placed on buses, trains, or other forms of public transportation.

CASH FLOW: The cash position in relation to all receipts and expenditures of an organization during a given period.

CENSUS DATA: Statistical information about a particular population, usually as collected by the U.S. Bureau of the Census.

CHANNELS OF DISTRIBUTION: The means by which a product or service moves from the producer to the consumer, either directly or through middlemen.

CHECKLIST: A device for the systematic evaluation (audit) of a marketing program (see Appendix A).

CHIEF EXECUTIVE: The lead marketer's immediate supervisor; most often the one responsible for all major functions relating to provision of service; synonyms are boss, superior.

CIRCULATION: The total distribution of free and/or purchased copies of a publication.

CLIENT: The organization or company that purchases such services as advertising agency creative advice or primary-research assistance.

CLOSED-END QUESTION: In research, questions phrased to elicit a direct answer from a respondent (e.g., yes/no, multiple choice).

CLOSING DATE: Deadline for delivery of final advertising copy to a medium in order to appear at a specified time.

CODING: In research, the assignment of responses to a particular numeric category for analysis purposes.

COMMUNITY RELATIONS: An aspect of public relations that involves continuing contact with various public-interest groups; requires initiative by agency to actively involve the public in important issues during various stages, not just a critical decision point or after the fact.

COMP.: See *Comprehensive*.

COMPETITION: Entities involved directly or indirectly in providing services similar to those provided by a particular organization.

COMPREHENSIVE: A layout resembling the finished advertisement, minus the finished copy; usually called "comp."

CONCEPT: The beginning stage of idea development; most often refers to advertising creative work in rough visual and headline form only.

CONCERT: To act in a unified manner (as musicians in a

musical concert) in a collaborative effort (especially implementation of a promotional program).

CONDUCTOR: Simile used to describe the manager or lead marketer (who should perform like a musical conductor) during program implementation.

CONFIDENCE LEVEL: In research, the estimated margin of error (e.g., described as plus/minus 5 percent) in quantitative research.

CONSULTANT: A supplier of professional advice or products (e.g., advertising materials) under contract to a client.

CONSUMER: The end user of services or products; a synonym is customer.

CONTEST: A type of promotional activity (e.g., a public contest to name a new public agency or service/product).

CONTINUITY: Effective flow in the implementation of a promotional campaign; also, repetition of the same basic theme, color, and graphics in a variety of advertising media; also, television, radio, and film production scripts.

CONTRACT: A formal agreement between two (or more) parties.

CONTROL: To have authority over the conduct of a process, project, or program; also, a technique for monitoring work progress.

CO-OP PROGRAM: An activity, usually between two parties or interest groups, which promotes their mutual interests (e.g., employer subsidy of monthly transit passes for their workers).

COORDINATION: The act of communicating among all affected individuals and/or groups during planning and implementation of a joint effort.

COPY: The written element of either the rough or finished advertisement.

COUNTER CARD: A self-standing promotional piece used alone, or as a dispenser for other advertising material on counters or shelves of appropriate offices or stores in the service area; one form of point-of-purchase (sale) display.

COUPON: Certificate offering discount in price of service or product; usually circulated as cut-out in print advertising or by mail.

CROSS-TABULATION: In research, the comparison of related categories of quantifiable information, such as usage related to the age of users of a service.

CROSS-TIME STUDY: In research, information gathered at successive points in time, using comparable methods and questions, in order to determine trends, successes, and areas needing corrective action; synonymous with tracking study.

CRT: Abbreviation for cathode ray tube, a video unit used in conjunction with data or word processing.

CUBICLE: A cell in a three-dimensional marketing matrix (see Figure 6).

CUSTOMER: Synonym for consumer.

CUSTOMER SERVICE: A fundamental marketing function relating to the handling of customer complaints and commendations, the provision of verbal and printed information, and the offer of special services designed to enhance customer convenience.

CYCLICAL: Descriptive of the marketing process that involves the phases of planning, implementation, and evaluation (usually over a one-year period) in a repetitive sequence.

DAY-PART: Division of broadcast media on-air time; A.M. drive, mid-day, and P.M. drive are radio examples; early fringe, prime, and late-night are television examples.

DELEGATION: Passing authority to act to a subordinate or, in some cases, to a peer; should be accompanied by accountability.

DELPHI TECHNIQUE: In research, a method for using the studied opinions of three or more experts on a subject to arrive at a consensus; often involves several iterations of responses.

DEMAND: The quantity of a service or product the market-place will absorb in a given time and under prevailing conditions.

DEMARKETING: Efforts to reduce demand for a service or product where such demand exceeds the supply (as in the promotion of energy conservation).

DEMOGRAPHIC: In segmentation—population's age, sex, income, education, household size, and so on.

DESIGN: The development of the characteristics of a particular service (product), such as the layout of a hiking-trail network; the detailing on paper of advertising concepts; the development of research methodologies.

DIARY: A qualitative method used to record individual responses to broadcast media programming under the Arbitron rating program; also used to research general topics.

DIRECT COMPETITION: A service or product similar in most respects to that offered by the primary organization.

DIRECT MAIL: An advertising medium using the postal service as the delivery means; pieces include a range of printed matter (e.g., postcards, brochures, and catalogues).

DISCIPLINE: A field of endeavor marked by recognized processes and standards.

DISCOUNT: In pricing, the offer of a reduced price as an incentive for greater trial and/or use of a service or product.

DISTRIBUTION: See *Channels of distribution.*

ELASTICITY: Related to demand for a service or product; demand is elastic when a price increase produces revenue increase; it is inelastic when a price increase produces a revenue decrease.

ELECTRONIC MAIL: The distribution of advertising messages or other communications via electronic means between two or more points (e.g., Federal Express's ZAP Mail).

ENVELOPE STUFFER: Advertising or public-information piece distributed with other mail, such as an electric-utility bill.

ENVIRONMENT: The circumstances in which work is conducted, including physical, spiritual, and emotional considerations.

EVALUATION: The third phase of the marketing process during which the results of planning and implementation are assessed and reported.

EVENTS: Activities, such as ribbon-cuttings, that are designed to call favorable attention to an organization.

EXTENDABLE: In relation to a promotional theme, the matter of whether a theme can have other applications, either through a modification of the words of the theme or its use in a variety of media (e.g., a television theme line carried through on a counter card).

FIELD WORK: In research, the period when interview responses or other data are gathered.

FLIGHT: One of a series of multimedia hits during a three-month promotional campaign wave, such as two-week flights of radio, with a one-week break between each.

FLIP CHART: An easel-mounted pad that is extremely useful for sketching ideas, focusing discussion, and communicating in small groups (from 3 to 12).

FLYERS: Single-sheet (usually 8½ by 11 inches) advertising or information piece.

FOCUS GROUP: In research, groups of diverse individuals brought together for in-depth, unscripted discussion about a particular subject; excellent to gain personal reactions but not conclusive evidence that can be generalized to the population (universe).

FORCED-CHOICE QUESTIONS: In research, a multiple-choice question that eliminates "no opinion," thus forcing the respondent to make a choice.

FORECASTING: Appraising the nature and magnitude of future trends over three to five years, based on historical trends and/or modeling of relevant factors.

FORMAT: A key consideration in packaging presentations (includes such considerations as the length, structure, content, and audio-visual aids—if any).

FOUR P'S: A classic summarization of the basic elements of marketing, including product, place (getting message to markets), promotion, and price.

FREQUENCY: The number of times an advertising message is delivered to an audience in a specified time period (see *Reach*).

FULL-SERVICE AGENCY: In advertising, an agency offering all client advisory, creative, production, and media-placement capabilities; may or may not include a research division.

FUNCTION: An aspect of marketing, such as public relations or research.

FUTURECASTING: Like forecasting, although for a longer-range (five years and beyond) period.

GEOGRAPHIC: In segmentation, the physical location of a particular population.

GOAL: A desired result requiring as a minimum three to five years to achieve; stated in general and usually nonquantified terms (e.g., to be recognized as the best zoo in the Midwest).

GOAL CONGRUENCE: An exercise among employees (usually management) in an organization to determine the similarity (or dissimilarity) of individual goals as they relate to the whole group.

GOVERNMENT RELATIONS: A facet of public relations that represents an organization before the various political bodies having governmental authority in all or part of the service area.

GRAPHIC ARTS: Activities involved in packaging and presenting the marketing message, including art, color effects, photography, copy, and reproduction.

GRAPHICS MANUAL: Produced by the graphic arts unit to depict standards for all visual elements relating to the organization.

GROUP: Synonym for division or section in a bureaucracy.

GROSS RATING POINTS: See *GRPs*.

GRPS: Abbreviation for gross rating points; in broadcast advertising, the scale used to indicate the number of total impressions delivered to a particular audience, without consideration to duplication; sometimes expressed as reach times frequency; usually referred to as "grips;" net rating points are unduplicated impressions.

HEAVY-UP: In media buying, to purchase more advertising in some medium, time period, or day-part than in others, or than originally intended.

HIT: The point at which media advertising is seen, heard, or distributed to the public.

HORIZON YEAR: In long-range (three to five years) planning, the last year of the plan.

HOUSEHOLD: A living unit for one or more persons; an element in demographic segmentation.

HOUSE ORGAN: An informational newsletter produced by an organization primarily for internal distribution and selected publics. (See *Newsletter.*)

IMAGE: The quality and nature of the public's perception of an organization.

IMPLEMENTATION: The second phase of the marketing process during which planning is put into action; synonymous with the promotional phase.

IMPRESSIONS: In advertising, the number of times a target audience sees or hears a particular message in a given period.

INCENTIVE: In promotion, a device used to stimulate demand, such as discount coupons (sometimes called premiums), free trips, or gifts.

INDIRECT COMPETITION: A service similar in certain basic respects to that offered by a primary organization (e.g., baseball in relation to a zoo; both are in competition for the entertainment dollar, though indirectly).

IN-HOUSE: Reference used most often to describe work that will be done by permanent employees of an organization, rather than by outside consultants.

INNOVATION: New and creative ways to achieve desired results in relation to objectives, resources, and policies.

INSERTION ORDER: Authorization from an advertising agency to a print medium to place an ad at a specified size, time, and rate.

INSTRUMENT: In research, synonym for questionnaire.

INTERCEPT INTERVIEW: In research, a method whereby the interviewer approaches the prospective respondent in a random manner in some public place, such as a shopping mall.

JARGON: The language of a particular field of endeavor; especially to be avoided when speaking or writing to those outside the field.

JOB DESCRIPTION: A written statement of functions and responsibilities associated with an organizational position.

KARATE CHOP: A term coined by the author to describe the effect of bringing all promotional elements to bear with maximum impact.

LABOR AGREEMENT: A contract between the management of an organization and a recognized labor union representing persons employed by the organization; relates to wages, benefits, work rules, and other compensation/ performance issues.

LABOR RELATIONS: The ongoing communications between the management of an organization and one or more labor unions representing employees of the organization; culminates in periodic negotiations for renewal of the labor agreement—which may or may not be achieved without hostile actions, such as work slowdowns, lockouts, or strikes.

LABOR UNION: A formal and recognized body of employees

in an organization whose purpose is to protect and enhance working conditions and compensation through on-going relations and contracts with the management.

LAYOUT: A drawing and/or mockup (dummy) of how an ad or publication would appear; also descriptive of the finished version of the ad or publication.

LIFE-CYCLE: Sales-volume pattern of a product or service from introduction through maturity, decline and, often, extinction.

LIST HOUSES: Firms that provide names, addresses, and labels for direct mail of advertising materials or telephone numbers for surveys; particularly useful in the targeting of selected segments.

LOBBYING: The process of pursuading governmental decision-makers to act in support of a particular organization's interests; open, honest, and direct communication are keys to success.

LOGO: Distinctive graphic or sound signature of an organization developed for use in advertising, free media, and internal purposes.

LONG-RANGE PLAN: Sets forth the marketing program three to five years ahead, from a base of the annual marketing plan (see Appendix B).

LOST CALL: The telephone call to an agency that was not answered because the caller got tired of hearing a busy signal or was disconnected; good telephone service is a *must* of customer relations.

MAILER: Synonym for direct mail.

MAILING LIST: The names and addresses of persons and/or groups to whom an advertiser desires to mail his or her message; usually segmented in some manner (e.g., geo-graphically by zip code, demographically by age group and light/heavy users of the service—or a combination of these).

MAIL QUESTIONNAIRE: In research, a printed list of ques-tions that is mailed to the respondent; must be less lengthy than the questionnaire administered by tele-phone or in person in order to gain sufficient response; should be accompanied by post-paid return envelope and promise of copy of survey results.

MANAGEMENT BY EXCEPTION: Also known as the "red flag" approach; involves identifying those activities that are not consistent with the marketing plans and taking appropriate action.

MANAGEMENT BY OBJECTIVES: See *MBO*.

MANAGEMENT INFORMATION SYSTEM: See *MIS*.

MANAGEMENT TEAM: The group composed of (usually) the administrative head (chief executive) of an organiza-tion and those reporting directly to him or her.

MANAGER: The person to whom this book is directed; syno-nym is lead marketer.

MARKET: Those who can benefit from a service or product and have the money to purchase it.

MARKETER: A term misused to describe those engaged in many of the functions of marketing (e.g., public rela-tions, sales, or advertising); the true marketer is a planner, implementer, and evaluator who orchestrates all of the marketing functions (and coordinates closely with all affected groups) to achieve the organization's goals and objectives, as expressed in the annual mar-keting plan and long-range plan.

MARKETING: All activities involved in transferring a service (product) from the producer to the customer; more than just research and advertising, this includes building demand for the service, evaluating the customer's response or lack of response, and reshaping the service, as necessary, to respond to low or changing demand.

MARKETING MIX: The combination of functions—and activities within each function—chosen to accomplish the marketing objectives.

MARKETING ORIENTATION: An attitude shared by every employee in an organization that the service (product) is being provided for the benefit of the customer, rather than the organization itself (an operations orientation).

MARKETING PLANNING: A process for organizing and communicating future marketing activities through the project plan, annual marketing plan, and long-range plan.

MARKET MATRIX: A three-dimensional diagram that permits various market segments for a particular service (product) to be arrayed against and compared with each other in order to determine the optimum mix of segments to be targeted (See *Figure 5*).

MARKET PENETRATION: The response of a specific market to the service (product) provided by an organization; expressed in terms of number of users (buyers) and market share (especially when there are one or more direct competitors).

MARKETPLACE: The geographic area(s) in which a service or product is offered; synonymous with service area.

MARKET POTENTIAL: The opportunity for increased penetration of one or more markets for a service or product; determined through forecasting and futurecasting and related marketing-planning activities.

MARKET SEGMENTATION: The subdivision of markets by geographic, demographic, psychographic, usage, or other characteristics; fundamental to target marketing.

MARKET SHARE: In an environment with one or more direct competitors, the portion of the market that uses (buys) an organization's service (product); expressed as a percentage of total use (sales).

MATURE: In relation to a service or product, the term used to describe its relative age in the marketplace; especially important to recognize when considering changes in long-successful services or products, or aspects relating to them. (See *Life-cycle*.)

MBO: Abbreviation for Management by Objectives, a concept used by most progressive organizations to relate its activities to measurable objectives; frequently tied to employee compensation in terms of salary progression, merit pay, or bonuses.

MEANS: Used here to describe both the media for transmitting and the channels for distributing an advertising or informational message to the marketplace.

MEDIA BUYER: The person who plans and accomplishes the purchase of advertising time or space from broadcast, print, or other media that sell advertising space (e.g., outdoor or transit); a large ad agency usually separates planners and buyers.

MEDIA MIX: The combination of advertising media selected to implement a promotional program or project.

MEDIA RELATIONS: That aspect of the public relations function involved with preparing news releases, photographs, and related materials for use by the editorial departments of various media; synonymous with public information as an organizational subunit.

MEDIA REP: Representative (salesperson) of an advertising medium.

MERCHANDISING: Activities of the producer or others in the channel of distribution to enhance customer acceptance of a service or product; retail-store displays are a well-known example.

MESSAGE: The content of the advertising communication; designed to emphasize the most attractive features of the service or product.

METHODOLOGY: In research, the techniques employed to extract information from respondents (e.g., telephone interviews, mail questionnaires, intercept interviews); also, the techniques used in designing and drawing samples.

MICROFICHE: Film on which large amounts of information is stored for reference use in libraries, information centers, and so on.

MILESTONE CHART: A single-sheet summary chart listing tasks to be performed on one axis and the spectrum of dates for the program or project in question on the other; the deadlines, and/or period for accomplishing each task are shown; this format portrays the total project work picture and flow in a clear and easily communicated manner (see Figure 9).

MIS: Abbreviation for management information system, a computer-based method of organizing and analyzing large amounts of data.

MULTIMEDIA: Short for multiple media in describing either a combination of advertising media or a presentation involving visual and sound elements.

MULTIPLE MEDIA: See *Multimedia.*

MULTIVARIATE: Statistical methods that relate three or

more variables (measures) at once, typically to predict or account for some single-criterion measure; involves multiple-regression/factor analysis.

NEWS CONFERENCE: An event at which one or more leaders of an organization interact with representatives of the media; can either be staged by the organization or called hastily in response to an issue the media wants to discuss.

NEWSLETTER: A letter-size sheet (usually one to four pages) published periodically by the public relations function of an organization to impart information internally and/or externally (see *House organ*); these vary widely in quality and content.

NEWSPAPER: A principal element of the print media; published daily, weekly, or monthly in the majority of cases with widely varying audiences, policies, and space rates.

NEWS RELEASE: A written communication (usually one to three pages) prepared by an organization for dissemination to the editorial departments of various media; often accompanied by photographs; frequently distributed in conjunction with a news conference.

NONPROFIT ORGANIZATIONS: Organizations established to deliver a public service (or product) at no profit above capital and operating expenses; often supported by public donations in some form.

NONUSER: In relation to a service, those who choose not to use it (like automobile drivers who never take the bus).

NOVELTY ADVERTISING: The vast array of items, ranging from pens and pencils to jackets and seat cushions, that have the name and/or logo of the sponsoring organization printed on them; synonymous with specialty advertising.

OBJECTIVE: An element and the heart of the annual marketing plan or an MBO program; states a desired end result of a work effort in measurable terms (i.e., quantity and deadline); an example would be to increase zoo attendance by 10 percent by the end of the current year.

OBJECTIVITY: In research, data free of researcher's bias.

OCCUPANT LIST: A mail list providing only the address of a residence, not the occupant's name; mail is addressed "Occupant" in lieu of a specific name.

OPEN-END QUESTION: In research, a form of question designed to give the respondents an opportunity to respond in their own words rather then be constrained by specific choices; contrasts with closed-end questions.

OPERATIONS ORIENTATION: An attitude among those in an organization that the seravice (product) is being provided for the benefit of the organization rather than the customer; contrasts with marketing orientation.

ORGANIZATION: A group formally established for a specific purpose; synonymous with agency (see *Bureaucracy*).

OUTDOOR ADVERTISING: An advertising medium placed in stationary locations along major roadways on billboards or other large backdrops; requires brief, eye-catching message because most viewers are in fast-moving vehicles.

PACKAGING: Used here primarily in reference to the contents and visual elements in the preparation of reports and presentations that communicate effectively in behalf of the marketing program; also used to describe the method of presenting or dispensing products/services to make them more attractive.

PAINTED BULLETIN: A form of outdoor advertising hand-painted on a large billboard or wall.

PANATONE MATCHING SYSTEM: See *PMS*.

PARAMETERS: The stated limits of an issue under consideration; in research, a descriptive measurement of a population, such as the standard deviation (amount of error) of a sample (see *Confidence level*).

PASTE-UP: A layout in which the type and photographic elements are affixed to a single sheet for reproduction.

PEERS: Those of equal position in a organization or engaged in like activities at a similar level outside the organization.

PENETRATION: The effectiveness of advertising in its impact on the general public; related to market penetration.

PERKS: A term used to describe extra benefits enjoyed by management personnel, such as a car or expense account; from perquisite.

PERSEVERANCE: To push onward toward specific goals in the face of setbacks, diversions, detractors, and other difficulties; indispensable to success in public-sector marketing.

PERSONAL INTERVIEWS: A technique for administering questionnaires to identified respondents.

PERT: Abbreviation for program evaluation and review technique; a more sophisticated critical-path scheduling method, usually done by computer.

PHASE: One of three major parts of the marketing cycle, which includes planning, implementation (promotion), and evaluation.

PLACE: To order advertising from an advertising medium.

PLACEMENT: In print advertising, the position of a particular ad in the publication and/or on the page, such as the first right-hand page above the fold.

PMS: Abbreviation for panatone matching system, a universal color-mixing code.

POINT-OF-PURCHASE DISPLAY: Any counter card, poster, banner, pennant, shelf-talker, dangler, header, or other device displayed where customers purchase a particular product or service.

POLICY: A rule of action (usually written) adopted by an organization to insure uniformity of response under recurring situations; fundamental to a bureaucracy.

POLICY BOARD: See *Board.*

POLICY-MAKERS: Those with authority to determine policy, either as an administrator or member of the board.

POSITIONING: An attempt by the producer of a service or product to achieve better acceptance by the target markets on the basis that their service/product fulfills certain wants or needs and is superior to the competition (e.g., largest, oldest, newest, friendliest); communicated in advertising copy or a theme—or both ("Fly the Friendly Skies" and "And the Drink of a New Generation" are well-known theme examples); powerful tool for gaining rapid acceptance of a service or product when properly executed.

POSITION POWER: The authority stemming from one's position in the bureaucracy; contrasted with personal power, which derives from individual qualities and capabilities.

POSTAL REGULATIONS: Policies governing mail advertising

that the marketer needs to become familiar with because of the growing use of this medium.

POSTTESTING: Testing of advertising after it has appeared to determine the respondents' awareness of it and attitudes about it; broadly, any measures taken after some experimental stimulus.

PRACTITIONER: One actively engaged in an activity, in this case as a marketer.

PRETESTING: Testing of advertising or survey questions before they appear to determine the respondents' reactions to them.

PRICING: Determining the amount to be charged for a particular service; also, discounts and other special price-related offerings; a difficult area for the public-sector marketer to gain or maintain needed control or strong influence.

PRIMARY RESEARCH: Research that requires the extraction of opinions from persons in a specific population by various methodologies, such as interviews or focus-group sessions; contrasts with secondary research, which is derived from available information.

PRINT MEDIA: A category of advertising media including principally newspapers and magazines.

PRIVATE SECTOR: Represented by business operated by investors for the purpose of making a profit; contrasts with the public sector, which comprises tax-supported organizations operated under budgets authorized by the governing board.

PROCESS: A systematic procedure for accomplishing work, either on a one-time basis or repetitively.

PRODUCT: All aspects of an organization's offering that the marketplace perceives to be of value; used as a synonym for service in the general sense; used alone in instances where the offering is a tangible item, such as a monthly bus pass.

PRODUCTIVITY: The level of results in relation to objectives, resources, and policies.

PROFESSIONAL: One who performs in a specific field to a high and consistent standard of quality.

PROGRAM: Used here to describe the annual promotional activity, launched after the planning phase, comprises a number of individual projects.

PROGRAM EVALUATION AND REVIEW TECHNIQUE: See *PERT*.

PROJECT: A well-defined activity with a specific purpose and time frame; component of a program.

PROJECT PLAN: Written outline describing the background and steps for accomplishing a project (see Appendix C).

PROMOTION: All paid and free media used to communicate the benefits of a service or product to the public at large and/or specific segments of the public (market).

PSA: Abbreviation for public service announcement, an informational message run at no cost by radio or television stations; usually run in the early-morning or late-night periods, which greatly diminishes its value.

PSYCHOGRAPHIC: In segmentation, a measure of the beliefs, interests, and attitudes of people in a particular population.

PUBLIC AFFAIRS: An aspect of the public relations function that has evolved to deal with issues where public- and private-sector policy are in potential conflict (e.g., the proposed annexation of an industrial plant by a city).

PUBLIC INFORMATION: See *Media relations*.

PUBLICITY: All free-media information generated in support of a service or product.

PUBLIC RELATIONS: All activities designed to build confidence and support for an organization among a variety of publics, including customers, taxpayers, suppliers, the community, and government; generally accomplished without use of paid media.

PUBLIC SECTOR: Represented by organizations financed in whole or in part by public tax dollars; works under budgets authorized by governing board; principally provides services (see Figure 1).

PUBLIC SERVICE ANNOUNCEMENT: See *PSA*.

PURCHASE ORDER: A form used to authorize the expenditure of funds for materials or services in an organization.

PYRAMIDAL STRUCTURE: Organizational form characterized by a narrower span of control (two or three subordinates reporting to the boss) (see Figure 4).

QUALITATIVE RESEARCH: Personal impressions about a service or product obtained by unscripted discussion with respondents through such methods as focus groups.

QUALITY: The degree of excellence of a person, service, or product; measured by consistent performance in relation to standards, objectives, and goals.

QUANTITATIVE RESEARCH: Statistical analysis of the marketplace obtained through structured methods like personal and telephone interviews guided by the use of a questionnaire; may also use secondary data.

QUESTIONNAIRE: A written document used to obtain orderly answers from a respondent; administered in person or over the telephone by a trained interviewer or by mail for completion and return.

RANDOM SAMPLE: In research, a form of sampling in which

each person in the sampling universe has a known opportunity of being selected.

RATE CARD: The statement of all rates charged by an advertising medium.

REACH: The number of individuals who are exposed to an advertising message.

REAL-TIME: In ADP, the instantaneous processing of data so that it can be used in a sustained or on-going activity.

RECALL: In research, a form of posttesting that asks respondents whether they remember what was said in an advertising message; also, an election to consider removal of a public official from office.

RECOGNITION: In research, a form of posttesting that asks respondents whether they remember having seen an advertising message.

RED FLAG: See *Management by exception.*

REFERENDUM: A public election on an issue or law.

RELIABILITY: In quantitative research, the ability to repeat a methodology with essentially the same results.

REPORT: A written or verbal summary of the status of a project or program.

REQUEST FOR PROPOSAL: See *RFP.*

REQUEST FOR QUALIFICATIONS: See *RFQ.*

RESEARCH: Careful and systematic study undertaken to determine facts about a particular subject; fundamental to the field of marketing.

RESEARCH HOUSE: Term for firm providing research services, including telephone banks and focus-group facilities.

RESPONDENT: One who replies (orally or by mail) to a research question.

RESPONSIBILITY MATRIX: A device used to array the functions assigned to a particular organizational group against a list of the staff personnel in order to clarify individual responsibilities for all involved; designed with functions/tasks along the vertical axis and the names along the horizontal.

REVERSE DIRECTORY: A telephone book alphabetized by street address rather than the occupant's name; useful in selecting direct-mail targets.

RFP: Abbreviation for request for proposal, a document issued by an organization to prospective bidders for a contract to supply services or materials.

RFQ: Abbreviation for request for qualifications, a document often sent in advance of an RFP to develop a field of qualified potential bidders on a contract.

ROLE PLAYING: A training technique in which the participants (either teachers or students or both) act out a situation, such as a sales person calling on a prospective customer.

ROTATION: The sequencing of a series of advertisements in an advertising medium.

RULE OF THUMB: A generalization that appears to have broad application, based on experience.

SALES PROMOTION: That aspect of promotion that involves such activities as displays, shows, and demonstrations to call attention to a service or product; often combined with the offer of incentives.

SAMPLE: In research, the scientific identification of a portion of the universe under study in such a manner that it accurately can be generalized to the whole.

SATURATION: A media advertising purchase designed to

maximize impact in a short period of time; may involve one (usually broadcast) or multiple media.

SCATTERATION STRUCTURE: A term coined by the author to describe the organizational form characterized by a broad span of control (4 to 10 or more) subordinates reporting to the chief executive). (See Figure 4.)

SCIENCE: Systematized knowledge based on observation, study, and experimentation; used here to describe certain aspects of marketing (e.g., research design, market segmentation, pricing, positioning, forecasting, media buying) (see *Art*).

SECONDARY RESEARCH: Research derived from available information, such as data compiled by agencies like the Bureau of the Census, local planning organizations, and newspaper libraries.

SELF-MAILER: Direct mail piece that does not require an envelope.

SERVICE: An activity deemed to be in the public interest and provided by an established organization or agency; characterized by interaction between a service provider and a service recipient; largest sector of the U.S. economy (see *Product*).

SERVICE AREA: See *Marketplace*.

SERVICE DESIGN: The development of the scope, level, and characteristics of the service to be provided; along with pricing—one of the difficult areas for the public-sector marketer to gain control and/or influence.

SHARE: See *Market share*.

SIGN-OFF STAMP: A stamp used to imprint a block on material ready for final production where the responsible individual or individuals can indicate their approval.

SIMPLICITY: Orderly, prompt, and focused approach to all

assignments; an absolute necessity in the complex and dynamic field of marketing.

SIMULATION MODELING: The use of mathematical formulas to approximate real-world conditions; employed for a variety of purposes from testing pricing alternatives to forecasting service usage.

SITUATION ANALYSIS: The foundation of the annual marketing plan; provides a base for formulating objectives and strategies through review and assessment of all relevant factors (e.g., the service, the marketplace, competition, and organizational resources).

SLOGAN: Sometimes used as a synonym for theme, which is the preferred term.

SNOWBALL: The term used to describe the momentum that arises from the cumulative effect of a series of successful actions and/or projects.

SPAN-OF-CONTROL: In a bureaucracy, the number of subordinates reporting to a superior (see *Pyramidal structure, Scatteration structure*).

SPECIALTY ADVERTISING: Synonymous with novelty advertising.

SPOT: Term for an advertisement in the broadcast media (i.e., radio/television spot); usually 30 to 60 seconds in length, although 15-second television spots are coming into vogue.

STAFF: All administrative personnel in a bureaucracy; also, used to describe specialists (e.g., legal, engineering in contrast to those in operating (line) departments).

STANDARDS: An established measurement of performance; standards for delivery of a public service to a large and diverse population are especially valuable as a means of maintaining fairness and equity.

STORYBOARD: An artist's concept of the visual elements and sequence of a television spot; accompanied by frame-by-frame copy.

STRATEGIES: The major actions undertaken to achieve an objective; like objectives, these should be expressed in measurable terms whenever possible (see *Objective*).

STRIKE: An action taken by a labor union against management; work stoppage usually occurs when an impasse is reached in contract negotiations.

STUDY: In research, a comprehensive effort to obtain research data, by the most appropriate methodologies, in regard to a specific subject.

STYLE MANUAL: Produced by the public information unit to set forth the standards for all written materials published by the organization.

SUBORDINATE: Employee reporting to the manager or lead marketer.

SUPERIOR: See *Chief executive.*

SUPPLIER: One who provides an organization with a service or materials under contract.

SURVEY: Sometimes used as a synonym for study, but generally less comprehensive.

SYNERGISM: The condition in which the impact of the whole becomes greater than the sum of its parts; achieved through skillful orchestration, whether the "parts" are individual employees or the various media in a campaign, or both.

SYSTEMATIC: An orderly approach to all aspects of (in this case) marketing, aided by standards, processes, and plans that help to ensure order and consistency over time.

TABULATION: In research, the counting of quantifiable results.

TACTICS: The activities undertaken to accomplish a strategy; like objectives and strategies, these should be expressed in measurable terms whenever possible (see *Objective, Strategies*).

TAKE-ONE: A counter card or other sales-promotion device designed to hold pamphlets or tear-off coupons.

TARGET MARKETING: Directing an advertising message to selected market segments by means of the positioning, media mix, and media buy employed.

TASK: A piece of work to be accomplished, usually as part of a larger project or program.

TAX: An assessment levied by a governmental body on all or a portion of a population; the primary (often sole) source of support for public-sector organizations.

TELEMARKETING: The sale of services or products by telephone.

THEME: A short statement in an advertising message that seeks to capture the essence of a service or product; designed to be remembered and repeated ("Uncle Sam Wants You!) (see *Positioning, Slogan*).

THEORY: A formulation of certain related principles regarding observed phenomena that have been verified to some degree; more advanced than a hypothesis and less so than a law.

TIMETABLES: Brochures produced by transit systems listing the route(s), schedule times and other information related to the bus service.

TIMING: Control of the schedule for implementing the elements of a project or program to achieve maximum impact and synergism (see *Nuance*).

TONE: The image and impressions conveyed by the content of all marketing media produced by an organization; the lead marketer has a responsibility to understand the subleties of color, style, graphics, and all audio-visual treatments that combine to convey a particular tone (See *Nuance*).

TRACKING STUDY: See *Cross-time study*.

TRADE PUBLICATIONS: Print media (e.g., magazines and tabloid newspapers) published for distribution to the members of a specific industry, such as travel planners.

TRADE SHOW: A popular sales-promotion activity; conducted at industry conventions to give suppliers an opportunity to display their wares.

TRANSIT ADVERTISING: A medium using large signs on the outside and smaller signs on the inside of public-transit vehicles; the sign space usually is leased by a private company which, in turn, sells the space to advertisers; revenues from the outside signs average about 90 percent of the total.

TURF: A bureaucratic term for an individual's real or perceived area(s) of authority in the organization; trespass at your own risk!

UNION: See *Labor union*.

UNIT: One of the sub-components of a marketing group.

UNIVERSE: In research, all individuals in the population to whom the sample results will be generalized.

USER: All those who use the service provided by an organization, ranging from association members to zoo goers.

VALIDITY: In quantitative research, the characteristic that data measure what they purport to measure; it is vital that questions be easily and consistently interpreted by all respondents.

VAL: Abbreviation for values and lifestyles, a method of psychographic segmentation developed by Stanford Research Institute.

VALUES AND LIFESTYLES: See VAL.

VIDEO: The visual element of a television broadcast; synonym for television.

VIDEOTAPE: Pictures on magnetic tape; similar to film but faster and less expensive to produce and it offers the benefit of immediate playback.

VIDEOTEXT: Computer-generated text for display on conventional television or CRT (see *Billboard*).

WASTE CIRCULATION: Distribution of an advertising message in areas where the service or product being advertised is not available or desirable for use or purchase.

WAVE: The major subelement of a promotional campaign, covering a period of one to three months and comprising several flights.

YARD SIGNS: A cardboard sign attached to a stake and placed in yards or along roadways to promote candidates or issues in a political campaign.

References

This list is provided for selective and in-depth reading in the general field of public-sector marketing and its more scientific aspects. The list comprises leading titles and readings in the respective areas.

GENERAL

Chase, Cochrane, and Kenneth L. Barasch. *Marketing Problem Solver,* 2d ed., Radner, PA: Chilton, 1977.

Dalrymple, Douglas J., and Leonard J. Parsons. *Marketing Management Text and Cases.* New York: Wiley, 1976.

Heskett, James L. *Marketing.* New York: Macmillan, 1976.

Kotler, Philip. *Marketing for Nonprofit Organizations,* Engelwood Cliffs, NJ: Prentice-Hall, 1975.

Lovelock, Christopher H., and Charles B. Weinberg. *Marketing for Public and Nonprofit Managers,* New York: Wiley, 1984.

Lovelock, Christopher H., and Charles B. Weinberg. *—Public and Nonprofit Marketing Cases and Readings,* New York: Wiley, 1984.

Lovelock, Christopher H., and Charles B. Weinberg. *—Services Marketing Texts, Cases, and Readings,* Engelwood Cliffs, NJ: Prentice-Hall, 1983.

Shapiro, Irving J. *Dictionary of Marketing Terms,* 4th ed., Totowa, NJ: Littlefield, Adams, 1981.

ADVERTISING

Naples, Michael J. *Effective Frequency: The Relationship Between Frequency and Advertising Effectiveness,* New York: Association of National Advertisers, 1979.

Ogilvy, David. *Ogilvy on Advertising,* New York: Wiley, 1983.

Seiden, Hank. *Advertising Pure and Simple,* New York: Amacom Executive Books, 1978.

Weilbacher, William M. *Advertising,* New York: Macmillan, 1979.

FORECASTING

Bonini, Charles P., and William A. Spurr. *A Statistical Analysis for Business Development,* Homewood, IL: Irwin, 1967.

Box, G. E. P., and G. M. Jenkins. *Time Series Analysis: Forecasting and Control,* Revised ed., Oakland, CA: Holden-Day, 1976.

Linstone, Harold A., and Murray Turoff, Eds., *The Delphi Method: Techniques and Applications,* Reading, MA: Addison-Wesley, 1975.

Wheelwright, Steven C., and Spyros Makridakis, 4th Ed., *Forecasting Methods for Managers,* New York: Wiley, 1985.

POSITIONING

Crawford, C. Merle. *New Product Management,* Homewood, IL: Irwin, 1983.

King, Stephen. *Developing New Products,* New York: Wiley, 1973.

Pessemeier, Edgar A. *Product Management: A Strategy on Organization,* New York: Wiley, 1977.

Trout, Jack. *Marketing Warfare,* New York: McGraw-Hill, 1985.

Urban, Glen L., and John R. Hauser. *Design and Marketing of New Products,* Engelwood Cliffs, NJ: Prentice-Hall, 1980.

PRICING

Forbis, John L., and Nitin T. Mehta. "Value-Based Strategies for Industrial Products." *Business Horizons,* May–June 1981.

Monroe, Kent B. *Pricing: Making Profitable Decisions,* New York: McGraw-Hill, 1979.

Nagle, Thomas. "Pricing as Creative Marketing." *Business Horizons,* July–August 1983.

Shapiro, Benson P., and Barbara B. Jackson. "Industrial Pricing to Meet Customer Needs." *Harvard Business Review,* November–December 1978.

RESEARCH

Aaker, David A., and George S. Day. *Marketing Research,* 2nd ed., New York: Wiley, 1983.

Boyd, Jr., Harper W., Ralph Westfall, and Stanley F. Stasch. *Marketing Research: Text and Cases,* 6th ed., Homewood, IL: Irwin, 1985.

Churchill, Jr., Gilbert A. *Marketing Research: Methodological Foundation,* Hinsdale, IL: Dryden Press, 1983.

Green, Paul E., and Donald S. Tull. *Research for Marketing Decisions,* 4th ed., Engelwood Cliffs, NJ: Prentice-Hall, 1978.

Index